Great Bible Stories for Children

—— Illustrated ——

Great Bible Stories
for Children

Paraphrased in Today's English

Text by R. Lane Easterly

Illustrated by Carlo Tora
and Alvaro Mairani

Royal Publishers, Inc.
Nashville, Tennessee 37202

This book will help children gain an appreciation for the wonderful stories of the Bible. The stories included in the book have been selected for their appeal to children as well as for their instructional value. They are written to be read easily and understood by children. Biblical source references appear at the end of each text.

May these stories help boys and girls of all faiths know more about God and Jesus; about living with other people and loving and worshipping God.

The Publishers

The Old Testament

The New Testament

The Old Testament

God Makes The World

Many, many years ago there was no world. There was nothing but God. No birds sang. No sun shone. No flowers bloomed. No children played. It was as black as midnight everywhere.

Then God began making the world a beautiful place for everyone to live in. "Let there be light," God said. The world became bright. God made the bright sunshine to shine during the day. He made the yellow moon and the bright stars to glow at night. Creation is the name we give to the time when God formed the world.

After God made day and night the heavy clouds still hung above. God said, "I will gather the waters together and cause dry land to appear." He called the dry places earth. He called the water the sea.

God saw that the world He was making was good, but He wanted it to become more beautiful. He said: "Let the earth bring forth grass and trees. Let the trees have fruit on them." God was pleased with the plants. The grass was green, flowers bloomed, and fruit hung from the trees.

God must have said, "The air will be a good place for living things, too." He made many birds. Some were red, some were blue, and some were yellow. The birds flew through the air, sang their songs, and built their nests in the trees. God decided to put living creatures in the water. He made big fish and little fish to swim about and live in the water.

But there were still no animals. "Now the earth needs animals on it," God must have said. He made the cattle and every other animal. The animals walked over the earth. They ate the grass and enjoyed the sunshine.

Genesis 1:1-25

The First Man and Woman

God was very pleased with all he had created. Everything was beautiful. However, God's work was not yet finished. In God's great plan there remained one special creation, different from all other living creatures. So God said "let us make a man. Let us make him in our own image, after our likeness, to rule over the earth and all the living creatures in it." So God took some dust from the earth and made a man. He named him Adam. Then God placed Adam in a beautiful garden—The Garden of Eden.

God placed many beautiful flowers and trees in the garden. Their fruit was good to eat. In the middle of the garden grew the Tree of Knowledge. God told Adam that he could eat the fruit of any tree in the garden, but that he could not eat any of the fruit from the Tree of Knowledge, for if he did, he would surely die.

Adam was very happy and loved God very much. But before long Adam became lonely. He needed a wife. God saw that this loneliness was not good for man so one day he caused Adam to fall into a deep sleep. Then, taking one of Adam's ribs, God made a woman. He named her Eve. Adam and Eve were very happy. They loved God and God loved them.

Then God looked at his world again and saw that it was perfect. The Earth had plants and animals and people. The sea had fish in it and birds filled the air. God was pleased and happy. Then God rested.

Genesis 1:26-31; 2

Adam and Eve Disobey God

One day while Eve was walking in the Garden of Eden, she passed the Tree of Knowledge. An evil serpent in the tree spoke to her. "Eve, tell me, can you eat fruit from every tree in the garden?" Eve said to the serpent, "We may eat the fruit of any tree except this tree, for God says if we eat from the Tree of Knowledge we will surely die." To this the sly serpent said, "No, you will not die. God does not want you to eat this fruit only because it will make you like God himself, knowing good from evil." The evil serpent could see that Eve was confused, so he tempted her even more. "Take a bite, Eve. See how good it tastes!" Eve did not want to make the serpent angry, so she took a bite and found that indeed it was very good. She ran to Adam saying, "Adam, taste this fruit, it is very good!" Adam then tasted the fruit. Suddenly things seemed different. They realized that they were naked; and they were ashamed. They tried to hide themselves deep in the garden, but God saw them and called to them.

"Adam and Eve, you have disobeyed me by eating the fruit of the Tree of Knowledge." God then told Adam and Eve that because of their sin they must leave the beautiful garden of Eden. From that day on they would have to earn their food by working very hard for it. Worst of all, he told Adam and Eve that because of them, man would not live forever and would die like all other creatures.

God also punished the evil serpent for tempting them. He made him crawl on his belly in the dust forever.

Genesis 3

The First Two Brothers

Adam and Eve had a son who was called Cain. Later they had a second son called Abel. When the two sons grew up, Abel was a shepherd and Cain was a farmer.

One day Cain and Abel went to make an altar and offer gifts to God. Abel brought gifts from his flock. God was pleased with his offering. But when Cain brought some of the things he had grown, God was not pleased.

Cain knew that God was not pleased with his gift. Cain was very angry. One day when he and Abel were out in a lonely field together, Cain killed his brother. Then he heard the voice of God saying to him, "Where is your brother Abel?" He was frightened and answered: "I do not know. Am I my brother's keeper?"

Then God said: "Cain, you killed your brother. From now on I will make you a wanderer, fleeing from all men. You will always have a hard time growing food to eat."

Cain said to God: "My punishment is too much for me. You have driven me out from my people. Everyone who sees me will do his best to kill me."

God felt sorry for Cain. God said to Cain, "No one will harm you." And then he placed his own mark on Cain's body so that whoever saw him would know that he was under God's protection.

Cain and his wife then took all they had and moved all the long, long way to the land of Nod, sometimes called the Land of Wandering.

Genesis 4:1-16

Noah Builds an Ark

It had been a long time since God had made the world and everything living upon it. There were many people on the earth, but they did not love God or obey him. God saw them do many things that were wrong. God said, "I will destroy everything that I made."

But there was one man who loved God. He and his family obeyed God. This man was Noah. Noah always tried to do what God wanted him to do. God spoke to Noah one day and said: "Noah, I am going to destroy all the people on the earth. I will send rain for forty days and nights. All the earth will be covered with water. But Noah, because you love me and try to obey me, I will not destroy you and your family."

Then God said: "I want you to build an ark. You must build it like I tell you. Before it begins to rain, take your wife and your three sons and their wives into this houseboat. I also want you to take two of some kinds of birds and animals into the ark. Take seven pairs of the animals and birds which men use most. You must also take plenty of food for all the people and animals."

God gave Noah the exact measurements that he should use when building the ark. Noah went to work at once. He followed the plan God had given him. When the people who lived nearby saw Noah and his sons building the ark, they laughed. "Look at Noah. Isn't he silly to build such a big boat on dry land?" they said to one another as they watched.

It took a long time to finish, but Noah and his sons worked and worked. At last, the big houseboat was ready. It was very long and three stories high. There was room for Noah, his wife, his three sons, and their wives. There

was also room for all the animals and birds that God had told Noah to take into the ark with him.

Then one day the sky grew very dark. God told Noah that it was time to go into the ark. Noah did as he was told. He and his family went into the ark. They led all the birds and animals into the ark as God had asked. When they were all safely inside, God shut the door of the big houseboat.

Genesis 6:5-22; 7:1-16

The Flood

After Noah and his family and all the birds and animals were safely inside the ark they waited for God to keep his promise. For seven days they waited. Then as God had said, the floods began.

The rain began to fall. Drop, drop, drop! It rained and rained and rained—for forty days and forty nights. Water began to cover the grass. Then the small trees were swallowed up in the floods. The animals and creatures that God had put upon the earth all died. Soon the houses and the towns and villages disappeared under the water. There was no hope for the people who lived in them. There was no place for them to go.

Still the floods came. Even the highest mountain and tallest trees were covered with water. The whole earth looked like the ocean.

The ark floated on top of the water. God was taking care of Noah just as he had promised he would. Inside Noah and his family were tossed about, but they were not afraid because they knew that God was with them.

At last the rain stopped. But Noah had to stay in the ark for many more days until the water had gone down. The winds began to blow and dry up the water. The warm sun began to shine. The water was lower and lower each day. Finally, the ark came to rest on top of Mount Ararat.

Noah opened the window of the ark and sent out a raven to see if the water had dried up. He also sent out a dove. When the raven and the dove came back, Noah knew that he must stay in the ark a little longer.

Seven days later, Noah sent out a dove again, but it did not return at once. All day Noah and his family waited for the dove to come back. When it was evening, the bird flew back with a leafy branch in its beak. Noah knew that the trees were appearing and that the land would soon be dry.

The next time Noah sent out the dove, it did not return at all because it had found dry land at last. Noah opened the door of the ark when he heard God saying: "Noah! Take your wife, your sons and their wives, and all the birds and animals out of the ark. Your family will be the first of a new generation. The children of your sons will have children and their children will have children also."

It was a happy day for Noah and his family. How glad they were to be on dry land again!

Genesis 7:17-24; 8:1-17

The Rainbow Promise

Noah and his family were very happy to leave the boat where they had lived for so long. It was good to see the sun again.

After Noah had released the animals, he said to his family: "God has been very good to us. Before we do anything for ourselves, let us thank him for keeping us safe and dry during the long days when the earth was covered with water." Noah and his family gathered stones and built an altar so they could worship and praise God.

God was pleased when he saw Noah and his family giving thanks. God said to Noah: "I will never again destroy the earth with water. Look at the clouds. I have placed my rainbow there as a sign. Each time you see the rainbow it will remind you of my promise. From now on as long as the earth remains, there will be summer and winter. There will be day and night. There will be a time to sow seed and a time to harvest the crops."

Noah looked at the sky. God had set a beautiful rainbow there. It shone in shades of red, orange, yellow, green, blue, indigo, and deep violet. It was the sign of God's promise.

Genesis 8:18-22; 9:1-17

The Tower of Babel

When Noah and his family came out of the ark they did what God had told them. They did not all stay in one place. It was not long before they had children and grandchildren. The families grew bigger and bigger. The families grew so large they were called tribes.

Even though all the tribes spoke one language and were really all the same family, they did not all think the same way. Some of the people were beginning to do wrong. They settled on a plain in the land of Shinar, about where Iran is today. They had an idea all their own. Since they knew how to make and bake bricks, they decided to build a great tower to reach right into heaven. They decided to build a great city around the tower. Then, they felt, they would be the greatest and the most wonderful of all people.

They baked their bricks and started building the city. The tower rose higher and higher. But something stopped them. God was watching them. God knew if they stayed together again like they had done before the flood, those with bad ways would soon rule over them, especially because they all spoke one language.

God changed their language. What trouble that brought! The brickmakers could not understand the builders. The builders could not understand the brickmakers. In a very short time the whole building work stopped. Those who spoke the same languages moved off together, each group in a different direction.

The great tower came to nothing. The place where they had tried to build it was given the name of "Babel," which means confusion.

Genesis 10; 11:1-9

Abram and Lot Make a Choice

In Ur, the city by the beautiful Euphrates River, there lived a family. Terah was the father, and his three sons were Abram, Nahor, and Haran. Haran had a son whose name was Lot.

One day God told Abram to get ready for a long journey. "Move away from this country and go to a land that I will show you. I will make you to be the beginning of a great nation. I will bless you and make your name famous."

Abram and his family packed their things and set out. They did not know the road or the name of the country to which God was taking them, but they knew God would keep his promise. They traveled north to a place called Haran. Then God told them to travel west and south until they came to the land of Canaan. The Canaanites were living in the land, but God made Abram a promise. "I am going to give all this land to your children and to your children's children."

They traveled on to a place called Bethel where Abram built an altar for a place to pray to God. By this time Abram had become a very rich man. He had many, many cattle and sheep, oxen, and camels. He had treasures of silver and gold. Lot was a rich man, too. His flocks and herds were very large.

Abram and Lot needed plenty of pasture land for all their animals. They soon found that they were too crowded on the land around the mountains near Bethel. Lot's shepherds and Abram's shepherds quarreled over the pasture lands and the water.

Abram called his nephew Lot to his tent. "Let's not have any fighting between our men or between you and me. Look, there is the land before you. Choose which section you want and take your men and your herds and go your way. You may have first choice."

"I choose the plain country," Lot decided.

So Abram stayed in the hill country and Lot and his people moved away to the green, green valley toward Sodom.

Genesis 13:6-18

Abraham, Sarah, and Isaac

After Lot and his people moved away, Abram, who still had no children, heard God speaking.

"Abram, I am the Almighty God. Stay close to me, and be a perfect man. You are going to be the father of many nations. No longer will your name be Abram, 'high father,' but Abraham, 'father of many.' Your wife Sarah will have a son."

Abraham laughed. "I am ninety-nine years old. Sarah is ninety. How can we have a child?"

"You will have a child and you are to name him Isaac. And I will keep my promise with him."

God did keep his promise. Sarah held her own baby in her arms. Abraham and Sarah named the baby Isaac. The name meant Laughter. "God has made me laugh," said Sarah. "Everyone who hears will laugh with me. Who would have said to Abraham that Sarah would have a baby?"

The home was happy because of the baby. When Isaac was old enough to eat with the grownups his father gave a great feast. All the household celebrated.

Genesis 17; 21:1-7

Abraham's Test

When Isaac was about fifteen years old God gave Abraham a test of his obedience and faithfulness. God spoke to Abraham: "Take Isaac, your only son, and go to a mountain in the land of Moriah. Offer Isaac to me as a burnt offering sacrifice."

How sad Abraham was to receive this command from God. But Abraham listened, because it was God who had spoken, and he trusted God. At the place God had told Abraham about, he and Isaac built the altar. They placed wood on top of it. Then Abraham fastened Isaac's hands and feet and laid him on the wood. After that came the awful moment. Abraham took a knife and lifted it up to kill his only son, Isaac.

But at that very moment a messenger of God spoke: "Abraham! Abraham! Do not touch Isaac. Now I know how much you love God and want to serve him. You have not kept back your only son from him."

A noise in the bushes attracted Abraham's attention. Abraham looked up. Right in front of him, caught by its horns in a thorn bush, was a ram. Together Abraham and Isaac used the ram for a sacrifice offering. They worshiped God there. Abraham knew that he could trust God no matter what happened.

Genesis 22:1-19

A Wife for Isaac

When Sarah died, Abraham knew that he would not live much longer. In those days the parents always found wives for their sons. Abraham called his oldest, most trusted servant to tell him how he must go about finding a wife for Isaac.

Abraham sent the servant all the way back to Haran to look for a wife for Isaac. Abraham's brother Nahor still lived in Haran. Abraham hoped that the servant would be able to find in that tribe a wife for Isaac.

When the servant eventually came to the country of Nahor, near the town of Haran, it was evening. He stopped beside the well outside the town. Soon the women would be coming out to get water. Before they came, the servant prayed that God would make the lady who should be Isaac's wife answer him in a special way when he spoke to the women. If he asked one of them to let down her jug into the water and give him water to drink, then the right one must not only give water to him but to his camels as well.

And Rebekah, the daughter of Bethuel, Abraham's nephew, did just that. After the servant had spoken with Rebekah she ran on ahead to tell her family what had happened.

When he came to Rebekah's house, the servant told her family why he had come. He explained who Abraham was. He gave them the presents Abraham had sent. The servant told how he had prayed to God to show him the lady who was to become Isaac's wife. And then he said he was sure that Rebekah was the right one. Her father, Bethuel, and her brother, Laban, were also sure it was God's will and that Rebekah must go back to be Isaac's wife.

On the evening that Rebekah and the servant arrived back near Abraham's tent, Isaac was out in the field. He saw the servant coming back. He went out to meet them. When he and Rebekah saw each other, they loved each other right away.

Soon they were married. For the first time since his mother died, Isaac was not lonely any more.

Genesis 24

Joseph and the Beautiful Coat

Joseph was one of twelve sons. His father was Jacob. They lived in the land of Canaan. Jacob was very fond of his son Joseph. Benjamin, the youngest brother looked up to Joseph, but his older brothers disliked him for bragging about the gifts his father gave him.

When Joseph was seventeen years old, Jacob gave him a coat made of many colors of cloth. It was a beautiful coat. Joseph's brothers became jealous and hated him. "Our father loves Joseph more than he loves us," they grumbled. "Look at that coat. It is finer than any of our coats."

One night Joseph had a dream. When he told his brothers about the dream the next day, they hated him even more. In his dream all the brothers had been cutting wheat in the fields and each one bound what he had cut into a bundle. Then Joseph's sheaf of wheat stood up and all the others bowed down to it.

A few nights later Joseph dreamed again. Once more he told his brothers what he had dreamed. This time he saw the sun and the moon and eleven stars bowing down to him. And then even his father was angry. "What is this?" Jacob said. "Am I and your mother and your brothers all to kneel before you?"

Later all the brothers except Joseph and Benjamin went out to look after sheep. When they had been away several days, Jacob sent out Joseph to see them and to find out how they were getting along.

As his brothers saw him coming toward them, but still a long way off, they decided that they would kill him. The brothers took Joseph's coat from him and then threw him into a hole. Then they noticed an Ishmaelite camel train on its way to Egypt with all kinds of spices to sell there. One of the brothers, Judah, had a plan. He suggested that they sell Joseph to the Ishmaelites to be sold again as a slave in Egypt.

The brothers took Joseph's coat and tore it. Then they dipped it in the blood of a goat they had killed. They sent this blood-stained coat back to Jacob. When Jacob saw the coat he was terribly upset. He believed that a wild animal had killed his favorite son.

Genesis 37

Joseph the Slave

When the merchants reached Egypt, they took Joseph to the slave market. Captain Potiphar, who was the head of the palace guard, found Joseph in the slave market. He liked Joseph the minute he saw him. Potiphar paid the price the traders asked for Joseph.

Joseph's life was different now. Once he had been the favorite son of a Hebrew chief. Now he was only a slave! Joseph, the country boy, was in Egypt, living in a big house full of servants in a city of big houses. At first he was angry and thought how wicked his brothers had been. But after a while he remembered the stories he had told and how boastful he had been. He asked God to forgive him and help him to be brave. Through all his troubles

Joseph remembered to pray to God as his father had taught him.

Joseph worked hard for Potiphar. As the years passed his master trusted him more and more. Joseph was careful and faithful. When he finished a job it was well done.

When he was old enough, Potiphar made Joseph head of all the servants in the house. Then Captain Potiphar made Joseph head of the work that was done outside the house in the fields. At last Joseph was promoted to be superintendent of all of Potiphar's business.

Then something terrible happened. Potiphar's wife told her husband lies about Joseph. Potiphar believed all his wife said and threw Joseph into prison. But Joseph knew he had done nothing wrong and prayed that God would help him.

Genesis 39:1-20

Joseph in Prison

In prison, Joseph was the same faithful, hard-working young man he had been in Potiphar's house. The keeper of the prison discovered that he had a good worker who could be trusted. He began to give Joseph jobs to do. The prison keeper put Joseph in charge of the other prisoners.

One day two new prisoners were put in the prison. One was Pharaoh's chief butler. The other was Pharaoh's chief baker. One night each of them had a dream.

The butler had seen a vine and the vine had three branches. Then he saw those branches producing branches of ripe grapes. He took those grapes and pressed out their juice into Pharaoh's cup which he had in his hand. Then he gave the cup to Pharaoh. Joseph listened to the dream and said, "The dream means that Pharaoh will send for you within three days and give you back your job. When you are back in the palace think of me and tell Pharaoh that I have been wrongly put into prison. I was even stolen away from the land of the Hebrews."

Then Joseph listened to the baker's dream. The baker had seen himself carrying three baskets on his head, one on top of the other. In the top basket there were all kinds of cakes and baked food, but birds flew down and ate. Joseph said: "This is what your dream means. In three days from now Pharaoh will send for you and will have you put to death."

Three days later it all came true. Pharaoh sent for his head butler and gave him back his old position. But he gave orders for the baker to be hanged.

In prison, Joseph waited and waited to hear from the butler. But the butler had forgotten. For nearly two years Joseph waited, hoping to be set free.

Then one night Pharaoh had a strange dream. None of the wise men could tell him what it meant. Suddenly the butler remembered Joseph and told Pharaoh all about the way his dream had been explained. Pharaoh ordered Joseph to be brought before him.

"I have dreamed a dream that no one can explain. I have heard about you and your cleverness in understanding dreams," said Pharaoh.

"God gives me understanding," Joseph answered.

Pharaoh began, "I was standing on the river bank when I saw seven cows coming up out of the water. They were fat and well-fed. They walked over into the meadow and began to graze. While I was watching, seven more cows came up out of the river. They were the poorest, sickest, scrawniest cows I ever saw. They ate up the good fat cows, and they were still just as scrawny as they were before. Next I dreamed that I saw a stalk of corn that had

seven good full ears. I saw another stalk with seven ears that had been parched dry by the hot wind from the desert. Those burnt, withered ears of corn ate up the good ears."

"God is showing Pharaoh what he is going to do," Joseph told him. "Both dreams mean the same thing. The seven fat cows and the seven good ears stand for seven years when the crops are going to be good, and everyone will have plenty to eat. The seven thin, sick cows and the seven dried-up ears of corn stand for the next seven years, when nothing is going to grow and people will starve.

Then Joseph made a suggestion to Pharaoh. Men should be appointed to put away some of the food during the plentiful years. Then there would be food for the famine years.

Pharaoh was amazed at what Joseph told him. Pharaoh was so impressed by Joseph's cleverness that he put him in charge of all the food supplies. He made Joseph the greatest ruler in all Egypt next to himself in importance.

Genesis 39:21-23; 40; 41:1-46

Joseph the Ruler

When Pharaoh made Joseph in charge of all the land of Egypt, he gave Joseph a ring. He ordered Joseph to be dressed in fine linen clothes and put a gold chain around his neck.

Joseph went right to work. He traveled over Egypt to find out how the crops were growing. He ordered the people to build huge warehouses. He organized men to collect the grain for storage, preparing for the famine which he knew would come. This went on for seven years. So much grain was stored in the warehouses that the officers gave up trying to measure it.

Then the good years ended. The years of famine came. There was no food to take home or to the market. People ate the last bit of food stored in their own homes. "What shall we do? Where shall we find food? Give us bread to eat," they begged Pharaoh.

"Go to Joseph. He will tell you what to do."

Joseph ordered the doors of the warehouses opened. Carefully and wisely he organized the work of giving out the grain. There was enough food for everyone, but none was wasted.

Joseph had his own family now. He had married an Egyptian girl. Her name was Asenath. The names Joseph gave to his two sons showed how happy he was. One was called Manasseh, which means Causing to Forget. The other was named Ephraim, which means Having Plenty.

Only Egypt had stored food for the famine years. Because Joseph had listened to what God said, Egypt had enough grain to be able to sell even to other countries.

Genesis 41:47-57

Joseph and His Brothers

Back in the land of Canaan there was hunger because of the famine. Jacob heard that the Egyptians had plenty of food to sell. Jacob had great riches, but no food. So Jacob sent ten of Joseph's brothers to Egypt to buy grain.

Only Benjamin, the youngest brother, was kept at home. Jacob was afraid that something might happen to him.

After a long journey through the desert, Joseph's brothers arrived in Egypt. They went straight to the governor in charge of the wheat stores. They did not know this man was their own brother, Joseph. They all bowed down to him—exactly as Joseph's dream many years before had said they would.

The brothers did not know him, but Joseph knew who they were. Still, he treated them as if they were strangers. "Where do you come from?" he asked them. "From Canaan, to buy food," they answered.

"You are just spies," Joseph said. "You have come to search for the weak places in the land."

"No, lord," they pleaded, "all we want is to buy food. We are all the sons of one man. We are all brothers. Our youngest brother is still at home with our father and one—well, one brother has disappeared. We only want to buy food. We are not spies."

Joseph would not listen to them. "I shall put you to the test. All of you, except one, will be kept in prison. The other brother must go and get your youngest brother. If he is not brought, then all the rest of you will be treated like spies."

For three days they were in prison. Then Joseph had them brought before him. He changed the whole plan. Only one of them would have to stay in prison while the rest went to get the youngest brother. Simeon was chosen to stay in Egypt and was taken to prison. The rest of the brothers were sent home.

That evening, when the brothers stopped for the night, one of the brothers opened his sack of grain to get a little food for his donkey. There he found the money that should have been left with Joseph. And there was money in the sacks of the other brothers as well. They were all afraid.

When they arrived at home they told their father Jacob all that had happened and that Simeon had been left behind. They told Jacob how the governor wanted them to bring their youngest brother. But Jacob cried: "Joseph is dead, Simeon has gone and now you want to take Benjamin away from me." He would not allow it.

Genesis 42

Benjamin's Cup

When the food brought from Egypt had nearly all been used, Jacob said to his sons, "Go to Egypt again and buy us more food."

Judah told his father: "Father, the man who sold us the food said he would have nothing more to do with us unless we brought our youngest brother with us. If you would let Benjamin go with us, then we will go to Egypt for food. If not, we cannot go."

"Benjamin shall go with you," Jacob promised.

Once more the brothers came to the place in Egypt where food was sold. Joseph saw them arrive, but he did not pay attention to them. Instead he sent his servant to take them to his home and to prepare a great feast.

When Joseph came home, the brothers bowed before him. They handed him the presents they had brought. Joseph was friendly, but did not say a word about being their brother. All he did was ask how they were. He asked how their father was. Then he looked at his own brother, Benjamin. He asked if this was the youngest brother they had told him about.

Joseph longed to tell his brothers who he was, but he wanted to be sure that they really had become better men.

He had a plan to test them. He ordered his servants to hide his silver cup in Benjamin's sack of grain.

The next morning, as soon as it was light, the brothers started on their way home. They were not far from the city when Joseph sent his servant after them. When the servant caught the brothers, he asked them how they could be so ungrateful as to have stolen Joseph's cup. The brothers denied having stolen anything. They did not know what was in their bags.

And then the cup was found. Sadly the brothers went back with the servant to face Joseph's anger. They threw themselves down in front of him. They promised to become his slaves.

Joseph told them to go home to their father, except the one in whose bag the cup had been found. Without Benjamin, they would not dare to go home. They pleaded with Joseph. Judah begged to be allowed to stay as a slave in place of Benjamin.

Joseph could not stand it any longer. He sent all the Egyptians out of the room. When they had gone, Joseph told his brothers who he was.

The brothers were afraid. They remembered what they had done to Joseph. But he said: "Do not be afraid. I came here as a slave, but God has made me a great man in the land. I still have much work to do. Because there is famine in our own land, you must go back home and get our father, Jacob, and all your families and your flocks. I will see to it that Pharaoh gives you a place to live."

Then he hugged and kissed all his brothers, especially Benjamin.

Genesis 43; 44; 45:1-24

Jacob Blesses Joseph's Sons

Joseph's brothers went back to their father in Canaan. They told him all about Joseph and of their invitation to go and live in Egypt. Jacob told them to prepare for the journey.

All the people and their flocks and herds began the long trip down into Egypt. When they reached Beer-sheba, Jacob built an altar of stones. He had not forgotten that he owed God the deepest thankfulness for giving him back Joseph once more. An offering of thanksgiving was made to God.

During the night, God came to Jacob in a dream: "Jacob, I am the God of your father. Do not be afraid of going down into Egypt. I shall be with you. You will see your son Joseph. There I will make of you a great nation. When the right time comes I shall bring that nation out of Egypt once more."

When Jacob and all the family came to Egypt, Joseph rode out to meet his father. Joseph took his father and five of his brothers to meet Pharaoh. Pharaoh gave them permission to move into the land of Goshen, the very rich land on the east side of the Nile River.

When Jacob was one hundred and forty-seven years old, he felt that the time of his death was coming near. When Joseph heard this, he took his two sons, Ephraim and Manasseh, and went to see Jacob so that he might bless them.

Jacob blessed all his own sons and Joseph's two sons. Joseph was surprised to hear Jacob giving a greater blessing to his younger son, Ephraim, than to the older son, Manasseh. Manasseh would become a great man and the father of a great tribe, but the greatness of Ephraim and his family would be much more.

So the grandfather gave his blessing to all the family, and he said to Joseph just before he died, "Promise that you will not bury me here in Egypt but back home in the family burying place with Abraham and Isaac."

Genesis 45:25-28; 46; 47; 48; 49:28-30

Moses in a Basket Boat

About three hundred years after the death of Joseph, a cruel Pharaoh ruled over the land of Egypt. He made slaves of the Israelites, or Hebrews as they were called by the Egyptians. The Pharaoh ordered his soldiers to kill the baby boys in every Hebrew family.

One Hebrew mother named Amram wove a basket out of bulrushes. She covered the basket inside and out with pitch to make it water-tight. Then she put her baby son in the basket and hid the basket among the bulrushes at the edge of the Nile River.

"The soldiers will never find him there," she told her daughter Miriam.

Amram went home to look after Aaron, her other son. Miriam stayed to watch over the baby from a little distance away. After watching for a while, Miriam heard some people coming. She saw that it was one of Pharaoh's daughters coming down to the river with her maids.

The princess saw the basket among the reeds. She sent one of the maids to get the basket. When it was opened and she saw the baby she said sadly, "He must be one of the Hebrew babies." She knew about the cruel order her father had made.

Then Miriam came out of her hiding place and said to the princess, "I will find one of the Hebrew women to take care of the baby for you if you want me to." The princess gave her permission. Then Miriam ran to get her mother.

"I want you to take this child and be his nurse. I will pay you your wages. Take care of him for me." The

princess laid the baby in his own mother's arms.

How glad Amram was to hear that. Now she knew the baby would be safe and he would not even have to be hidden.

As soon as he was old enough, the princess sent for the child. His mother took him to the palace, and there he grew up as the princess' adopted son. He was given the name of Moses which meant that he had been taken out of the water.

Exodus 1; 2:1-10

Moses Runs Away From the Palace

Moses became an Egyptian prince and lived in the palace. He had slaves to wait on him. He learned all about the heathen gods worshiped by the Egyptians, but he had also learned about the Lord God, Jehovah, from his Hebrew parents.

Moses was a kind, thoughtful boy, but quick tempered. One day, when Moses had grown into a young man, he was out watching how badly the Hebrew slaves were being treated by the Egyptians. The Hebrew slaves worked in the brick fields in the heat of the sun. On this day he saw an Egyptian beating an Israelite workman. Moses was so angry that, after looking around to see if anyone was watching, he killed the Egyptian and buried him in the sand.

The next day he came across two Israelites fighting. He asked one of the men, "Why do you hit your Israelite brother?" The man said, "Who made you a prince and a judge over us? Do you plan to kill me as you did the Egyptian?"

When Moses heard this he was afraid. He knew that

when Pharaoh heard what he had done his own life would be in danger.

Pharaoh did hear. At once he sent out his soldiers to arrest Moses. But Moses fled from Egypt to hide in the land of Midian. Midian was a desert land and the people who lived there were shepherds. Moses wandered through the desert, wondering what would happen to him in such a terrible place.

Exodus 2:11-22

God Calls Moses

One day Moses was out in the desert with sheep near Mount Horeb. Suddenly he saw a thorn bush on fire. Moses went over to look at the bush. The bush kept burning and did not burn out. Moses was puzzled and went nearer to look more closely.

Suddenly as he watched, a voice called to Moses out of the bush. "Moses! Moses!" Moses answered, "Here I am."

The voice was coming straight from the fire. "Do not come near, Moses. Take off your shoes because the ground where you are standing is holy ground." Moses did as he was told. He was afraid.

Then the voice spoke again, "I am the God of your father, the God of Abraham, the God of Isaac, and the God of Jacob." Immediately Moses hid his face. He was afraid to even look at the fire. Then God spoke again: "I have seen the hardships of my people who are in Egypt. I have come now to free them from the cruel Egyptians and to bring them to a rich new land. I mean the land of Canaan which I promised their forefathers. Now, Moses, I want you to go to Pharaoh. Get my people away from him and bring the children of Israel out of Egypt."

Then God made a promise to be with Moses and give him all the strength he needed. God told Moses that when the people came out of Egypt they must travel to Mount Horeb. There they must worship God.

But Moses still hesitated. He had another question to ask: "When I go to the children of Israel and tell them that the God of their fathers has sent me to them they will ask his name. What shall I answer them?"

God answered Moses, "I AM THAT I AM. This is what you must say to the children of Israel. I AM has sent me to you."

Exodus 2:23-25; 3; 4:1-17

Moses Leads His People to Freedom

God told Moses to go to his own people in Egypt. There he must gather all the leaders of families together and explain to them why God had sent him. Moses was frightened and wished that God would choose somebody else. God promised that his brother Aaron would go with Moses and be his spokesman.

Moses went back to Egypt. As God had said, Aaron came out to meet Moses. Moses told Aaron all that God had said. Then they went and gathered all the leaders of Israel and gave them God's message.

Once they had spoken to the leaders of their own people, Moses and Aaron made their way to Pharaoh's palace. They went to do as God had said. They asked that the Israelites be allowed to travel out into the desert to worship there.

Pharaoh said: "Who is the Lord that I should listen to him? I do not know the Lord and I will not let Israel go." He told the overseers of the workmen to make the Israelites work even harder than before.

Moses was discouraged. But God spoke to Moses again and brought him once more the promise that Pharaoh would let the people of Israel go and he would lead them to the Promised Land.

The next morning Moses and Aaron went again to Pharaoh. But Pharaoh still would not listen to God's servants.

God sent Moses and Aaron again to tell Pharaoh that the Lord God of the Israelite people had sent them to ask him to free God's people so that they could worship him in the wilderness. This time they added a special warning. Aaron stretched out Moses' stick over the water in the river. The water turned to blood and the Egyptians could not drink it. For seven days it stayed like that. The people had to dig holes for drinking water away from the river.

Still Pharaoh would not do as Moses asked. This time God sent a plague of frogs which covered the land. Pharaoh begged Moses and Aaron to ask God to take away the frogs. He promised he would do as God demanded. But as soon as the frogs had disappeared, Pharaoh broke his promise.

Then God sent a plague of gnats which swarmed over every man and animal in the land. After the gnats came a plague of flies. Again Pharaoh promised to release the Hebrew slaves if God would take away the flies. As soon as this had been done Pharaoh refused to keep his promise.

After the flies came a plague on cattle. Then came a plague of sores on people and animals, then a plague of hail and storms, but Pharaoh still would not give in. Then a plague of locusts settled over Egypt and ate all the plants and the fruit of the trees which the hail had left. This time Pharaoh promised he would keep his word if

God would only take away the locusts. But as usual Pharaoh forgot all about his promise when God gave a strong west wind to take away the locusts.

Then God sent a plague of darkness which covered the land for three whole days. Again Pharaoh was quick with his promise until the plague was taken away. But this time he became very unpleasant. He told Moses and Aaron to leave the land immediately. Pharaoh said: "Get away from me. Never come near me again, for the day you do I will have you put to death."

Then came the last plague, the worst of them all. God told Moses: "About midnight, all the oldest sons in the land of Egypt shall die. Every Israelite family must prepare itself in a special way."

The Israelites were told to prepare a meal of roasted lamb, and bread without yeast. They were to dip a bunch of herbs in the lamb's blood and make marks on the doorposts and across the top of the door. They were told to stay indoors until the morning. When God saw the blood on the houses, those houses would be safe.

That night was one of terror in the land of Egypt. There was not a single home where there was not a son dead. Even Pharaoh's palace did not escape. Only the Israelites who had listened to what God had told them to do had escaped the touch of death.

This time Pharaoh was in a hurry to keep his promise. He told Moses to take the people of Israel, and their flocks and herds, out of Egypt as quickly as he could.

So the children of Israel left Egypt four hundred and thirty years after Jacob and his family had entered it. There were about six hundred thousand men, besides the women and children. God watched over them all. With Moses leading, they went toward the Red Sea. The Lord

went before them in a pillar of cloud by day to lead them. By night he gave them a pillar of fire to give them light.

When Pharaoh knew that the Israelites had gone and he had lost his valuable slaves, he called his army to go after the Israelites.

The Israelites were frightened when they saw the Egyptians following them, but God was still with them. When they came to the sea, Moses lifted his rod and stretched his hand over the sea. The water divided and the people of Israel passed safely through. When the Egyptians tried to follow, Moses again stretched out his rod and the waters came rushing back, covering the chariots and drowning the Egyptian soldiers.

God had saved the Israelite people and they believed in him. They trusted his servant Moses.

Exodus 4:14-31; 5 to 15:1-21

The Ten Commandments

Three months after the Israelites had left Egypt, they came to a mountain called Sinai. At this place God gave His Law to His people so that they would always know how to live together.

Moses climbed the mountain to receive the message for the people. There the Law was carved on two tablets of stone so that God's people would never be able to forget it. The tablets said: (1) You shall have no other gods except me. (2) You shall not have any carved likeness of anything in heaven or earth, or in the sea, to kneel before it or worship it. (3) You shall not use the name of the Lord your God in vain. (4) Remember to keep holy the Sabbath day. (5) Honor and respect your father and your mother. (6) You must not murder. (7) You must not commit adultery. (8) You may not steal. (9) You must

not bring false witness against your neighbor. (10) You must not covet.

While Moses was with God on the top of Mount Sinai, there was something unpleasant happening down in the Israelite camp. The people were melting all the golden ornaments and jewelry they had. They were making a golden calf and building an altar.

God knew what was happening and He was angry. He told Moses there was only one thing to be done. The nation must be destroyed. But Moses begged God not to treat them so harshly.

Then Moses turned and went down the mountain with the two tablets of Law in his hands. From a long way off he could hear the noise, but when he saw what was going on he was so angry that he threw down the tablets of stone. They broke into pieces. Then he took the golden calf and burned it. He ground the burned image to powder and threw the powder into water and made the people drink it.

Then Moses told the people to beg God to forgive them. He returned to Mount Sinai to pray for them. God told Moses to again take two pieces of stone. Once again God carved out the Law on the stones. When Moses went back to the people this time, the skin of his face shone like the sun.

Exodus 19; 20:1-20; 24:12-13; 31:18; 32; 34

The Battle of Jericho

When Moses became an old, old man, God chose a new captain of the Israelites. His name was Joshua.

"Be strong and fearless," God told Joshua. "Listen to me. Obey me, and you will win every war. Whatever happens you will know that I am beside you."

The first thing Joshua did was to call a meeting of his officers. "Tell the people to get food ready and pack up to travel," Joshua said. "We are going to cross the Jordan River and move into the country God has promised to give us."

Across the river was Jericho, a city with a king, an army, and high, strong walls to protect it. Joshua needed to find out how strong the wall really was. While the people were packing, he ordered two spies to see what they could find out.

The two men slipped through the city gates that were open in the daytime. They came to a house that was built right on the city wall. There they met a friendly woman named Rahab. Rahab hid the two men on the roof. "I know all about you," Rahab said. "I know that God has given you this land. I heard how God helped you cross the Red Sea when you escaped from Egypt. I know how strong you are. I know your God is the true God of all the heaven and earth. The whole city is afraid. No one here is really going to fight you."

"Promise not to tell anyone you saw us, and we will help you," the spies told Rahab. "Mark your window with a red cord so that when we come back we will know where you are. We will see that everyone in this house is safe."

Then Rahab showed them how to escape from the city even though the gates were locked for the night. She let them down by a rope through the window so that they were outside the city wall.

Two days later they made their report to Joshua. "God has already given us the land. The people have heard about us and they are afraid. They will not even try to fight us."

Joshua gave his orders. "Forward!"

The long line of people began their march. Straight toward the river they walked. As soon as their feet were wet, the water of the river piled up and stopped. The road across became dry. God was showing them the way. Finally everyone was safe on the other side.

Joshua stood outside Jericho looking at the high walls. "Jericho is yours. But keep none of the treasure you find for yourselves," God told Joshua. "This is what you must do."

Joshua listened carefully to the plan for capturing the strong city. Then he obeyed without asking a single question.

Early in the morning the attack began. First the soldiers lined up. Then came the priests carrying trumpets made of sheep's horns. Behind them other priests carried the golden ark of God's promise. The rear guard of soldiers was last.

"Forward, march!" Once around the city wall they marched. The only sounds were the music of the trumpets and the sound of the marching feet.

The next day they marched around the city again. For six days they marched just once around the city. There was no sound but the trumpets and the marching feet.

Just as it began to be light on the seventh morning the army and the priests formed again. "Forward, march!" ordered Joshua. There was no sound but the trumpets and the marching feet. Six times they marched around Jericho's wall.

"Ready, march! And shout!" Joshua ordered the soldiers and all the people.

The noise of shouting and trumpets and marching feet boomed outside the high-walled city as the Israelites marched round for the seventh time that morning.

And when they did, the walls of the city fell down, except the part on which Rahab's house was built. The great, strong city of Jericho was wide open to Joshua's army.

Joshua 5:10-15; 6

Joshua Remembers Caleb

For seven years Joshua led the Israelites as they fought in their new homeland. Thirty-one kings had been conquered. The time had come to divide the land among the tribes. It was time for the families to settle down on their own land, to build their houses, and to plant their crops.

One day while Joshua was dividing the land, an old man came to Joshua. The man was Caleb. More than forty years before, Caleb and Joshua had been sent out by Moses to spy over the border of the Promised Land.

"Remember what Moses said when you and I were not afraid to tell the truth?" Caleb began. "He promised me then that I was to have some land."

Now Caleb was eighty-five years old. As old as he was, he was still strong. He felt he was still just as strong as he had been when he went into Canaan as a spy. Now he wanted land on which to farm.

"Remember where we found the giants of Anak? Let me have the mountain where the giants live. This will be my home," Caleb told Joshua. "If God will help me, I will drive them all out."

When Joshua gave him the permission he wanted, Caleb led his soldiers up the mountain where the giants lived. He drove them out and took over the land he had chosen.

Joshua 13 to 21

Gideon

After forty years of peace, the Israelites began disobeying God's commandments. God had to punish them again. This time they had to suffer the attacks of the Midianites.

The Midianites were desert dwellers from east of Jordan. Every year when the Israelites' crops were ready to harvest, the Midianites rushed in and stole everything. They even brought their camels, sheep, and cattle, and allowed them to eat up all the grass. There were so many of the Midianites that the Israelites had to hide from them in caves or among the rocks in the mountains.

God made it clear to the Israelites why these things were happening to them. He sent a prophet to remind them of all he had done for their people in bringing them out of Egypt and into the land of Canaan.

One day one of the Israelites, Gideon, was at work

threshing wheat. Suddenly, sitting next to where he worked, there was an angel from God. The angel spoke to him: "Do not be afraid! Go out in strength to help your people. You will save them from the Midianites. Do not think you are alone in the fight. I shall be with you."

God told Gideon there were too many Israelite soldiers. If they defeated the Midianites they would think it was by their own strength they had done it and would forget all about God again.

Gideon talked to the soldiers. He told them that everyone who was the slightest bit nervous must go back home. Only ten thousand stayed. But God said there were still too many.

God told Gideon to bring the soldiers down to the riverbank. Gideon should tell the soldiers to drink water from the stream. Almost every one of them knelt down to drink. Only three hundred scooped up water with their hands. Those were the men God chose. They kept themselves ready to fight even while they were drinking.

Gideon prepared the three hundred for the battle. They were divided into three companies. Every man was given a trumpet, an empty jar, and a lamp to put in the jar. Then the lamps were lit inside the jars so that their light could not be seen. The soldiers then crept down until they were close to the Midianite camp.

Each of the three companies moved around to a different side of the camp. Then suddenly, at a signal from Gideon, they all blew their trumpets and smashed the jars and rushed into the camp with their lights showing and shouting: "The sword of the Lord and of Gideon."

The Midianites were so terrified they did not even fight. They ran as fast as they could.

Judges 6:1-40; 7:1-25

A Strong Fighter

In the land of Dan, alongside the country of the Philistines, lived a man called Manoah. One day an angel told Manoah's wife that she would have a son. The angel said that the son would begin to save his people from the Philistines. As long as he lived his hair must never be cut.

When the baby was born, he was named Samson. He grew up to become an extremely strong man. One day as he was traveling through the country a lion attacked him. With his bare hands Samson tore the animal in pieces and left the body lying on the ground.

Not long afterward he came that way again. He found that a swarm of bees had settled in the lion's body, and that it was full of honey. Samson tore off pieces of honeycomb and ate it as he walked along.

Samson made up a riddle. "Out of the eater came something to eat, and out of the strong came something sweet."

No one could guess the answer until he gave a hint. Then they knew. "What is sweeter than honey, and what is stronger than a lion?"

Everyone in all the land had heard how Samson fought against the Philistines even though he had been tied in strong ropes. Everyone in the land had heard how the Philistines had locked Samson

in the city. But at midnight Samson slipped down to the heavy, locked gate in the city wall. He pulled up the gate, post and all, and put them on his shoulders. Then he carried the heavy gate to the top of a hill. When the Philistines went to look for him, Samson was gone.

Judges 13 to 16:3

Samson Loses His Strength

Samson loved a woman named Delilah. The Philistines knew Samson loved her even though she was a Philistine. The Philistines begged Delilah to find out the secret of why Samson was so strong.

The Philistines offered Delilah eleven hundred pieces of silver if she would find out why Samson was so strong.

"If they do one thing," said Samson, "I'll be like any other man. Tell them to bind me with seven strong new bowstrings that have never been used."

So Delilah let him be bound tight with the seven new bowstrings. Samson's strong arms burst the seven new bowstrings like threads and he was free.

"You tricked me. Now tell me what really is the secret," Delilah begged.

"Tell them to bind me with new ropes," said Samson, "Then I will be as weak as any other man."

So Delilah let him be bound with new ropes. Samson burst the ropes like string and he was free.

"O Samson, tell me what really will hold you," cried Delilah.

"Weave my hair into the cloth that is being woven on the loom," Samson told Delilah. Then Samson went to sleep.

Delilah wove his hair into the cloth on the loom,

but Samson tossed his head and went away, cloth, loom, and all.

After that Delilah pouted and begged and worried Samson until he told the secret. "I am strong because I am a servant of God. My long hair is the sign of my promises to God. If my hair should ever be cut, my strength would be gone."

One day while Samson was sleeping, Delilah called for a Philistine to come and cut off his long hair. When he woke up, Samson's strength was gone.

Then the Philistines put heavy chains on Samson's arms and legs. They put out his eyes, making Samson blind.

"Let's celebrate," the Philistines said. "Dagon, our god, gave Samson to us."

All the important Philistines came to the celebration. They crowded into the court of the temple. Samson was brought in so that they could laugh at the helpless blind man who had once been so strong.

A little boy led Samson into the temple. The Philistines were so busy enjoying themselves that they did not notice Samson's hair had grown while he had been in prison.

"Put my hands on the pillars," Samson whispered to the boy. Then Samson prayed to God. "God, remember me. Make me strong. Let me fight the Philistines once more. I am ready to die with them."

Samson pushed with all his strength. The pillars began to give way. They crashed to the ground. The walls and the roof fell down on the people. Thousands of the Philistines were killed. And Samson died, too, in the ruined building.

Judges 16:4-31

Naomi Leaves Bethlehem

During the time when the judges ruled Israel, there was a famine. People were starving, even in Bethlehem. But in Moab there was plenty to eat.

One Israelite, called Elimelech, took his wife Naomi and their two sons and went to live in Moab. There Elimelech died. The sons married Moabite women, Orpah and Ruth. For ten years Naomi lived happily with her sons and daughters-in-law. Then sad times came. Both the sons died and only the women were left.

Naomi made up her mind that she must go back to her own country of Bethlehem. She had heard that the famine had ended there.

Her daughters-in-law were sad that Naomi was leaving them. They felt they must go with her as far as they could. When Naomi set out on her journey they started off with her to keep her company until she crossed over the Jordan River back into Israel.

After they had gone a little way, Naomi stopped. She told Orpah and Ruth that it was time for them to return to their families. She lovingly said goodbye, and prayed that God would be as kind to them as they had been to her sons and to her.

Slowly Orpah turned away and started on the journey home. But Ruth put her arms around Naomi and cried: "Do not ask me to leave you. Let me follow you. Where you stay I will stay. Your people shall be my people. Your God shall be my God."

Naomi tried her best to persuade Ruth to return with Orpah, but in the end she saw that it would not help. She said no more, and on they walked together, the old Israelite woman and her daughter-in-law.

It only took a few days' walk for them to get back to Bethlehem where Naomi had lived until the bad days of the famine. How surprised the people of Bethlehem were to see Naomi back again!

Ruth 1

Ruth Gathers Grain

Naomi and Ruth were very poor. They had no money. They needed food badly.

When they came to Bethlehem it was in the early summer. All the farmers and their workers were busy in the fields harvesting the barley crop. There was an old law about the harvest. When there was food, all must share, even the poor who had no land. This was the law of the gleaners. "When you harvest grain, leave a little in the corners and at the end of the rows. If you drop an armful, let it stay where it is."

So Ruth went down to work in the fields. She happened to go the fields of a farmer named Boaz. Boaz went out to check on his harvesters. He saw Ruth and asked who she was.

Boaz went up to Ruth and said kindly, "Stay here and keep close to my harvesters. You may follow them as they gather. When you are thirsty, you may have water from our water jars."

"Why are you so kind to me? I am only a foreigner," Ruth said to Boaz.

Boaz smiled, "I know about the kindness you have shown to your mother-in-law. I know how you have left your own land and your father and mother to come and care for Naomi."

Ruth went back to her work. Boaz quietly told his workers to pull some barley out of the bundles and drop handfuls on purpose for her to pick up.

Ruth worked in the field until evening. When she took the grain home, Naomi was surprised to see so much.

"Where have you been working today to gather so much grain?" Naomi asked.

Ruth told her everything that had happened and the name of the friendly man in whose fields she had worked.

"Boaz is a relative of ours," Naomi said excitedly. "The Lord is good to us."

Everyday until the end of the barley and wheat harvests Ruth worked in the fields belonging to Boaz. She collected enough food to make sure she and Naomi would have enough to keep them through the winter.

Ruth 2; Leviticus 19:9

Ruth and Boaz

The Israelites had a custom that if a man died without leaving children and he owned land, the nearest relative had the right to buy that land and marry the widow.

Naomi had a plan. She said to Ruth, "It is time you had a home of your own. Boaz can help you. Tonight he will be working on the threshing floor beating the chaff from the wheat. Put on your best clothes and go and see him there. Wait until he finishes his supper and then when he lies down to sleep, find a place near him where you can lie down."

It was very dark. Quietly Ruth slipped past the stacks of grain and lay down on the ground at Boaz's feet.

"Who's there?" he whispered.

"I'm Ruth, and you are my cousin. You have the right to buy our land."

"Don't worry, Ruth. I will do all that I can, but there is a man who is even closer kin to you than I. In the morning I will go and see him."

So Ruth slept on the threshing floor. In the morning while it was still dark, Ruth got up to go back home. In his usual kind way, Boaz would not let her go away empty handed. He poured six measures of grain on the sheet on which she had slept. Off Ruth went to tell her news to Naomi.

Naomi nodded, smiling, "Wait a little while. Boaz will attend to this business today."

That morning Boaz went to the gate of the town. The man he wanted to see came along. Boaz saw the man coming and called to him. Then he asked ten of the wise old men of the town to stop and be witnesses.

Then Boaz said: "Naomi, who is kin to us, has come back from Moab. Her husband Elimelech died while they were living there. So did her two sons. Now she only has her daughter-in-law, Ruth, to take care of her. Naomi wishes to sell the land which belonged to her husband. It is your right to buy that land. But if you buy the land from Naomi you must also marry Ruth.

"The land I would gladly buy, but I cannot marry Ruth," the cousin said when he heard Boaz' story.

Then Boaz said to the people, "You are witnesses that today I have bought from Naomi all that belonged to Elimelech and his sons, and I am buying the right to marry Ruth."

"We are witnesses. May the Lord bless your home," said all the people.

So Ruth and Boaz were married. The sad and lonely

days were forgotten. The day a son was born in the home of Boaz and Ruth, all the neighbors came to celebrate with Naomi.

Ruth 3 and 4

Hannah Prays for a Son

After the death of Samson, the next judge of Israel was Eli. Eli was also the high priest in the tabernacle at Shiloh. He and his two sons were in charge of the sacrifice offerings the people brought to God.

Hannah and her husband, Elkanah, lived at Ramah. They had no children. Each year they went up to the tabernacle to bring an offering to God. One year, Hannah slipped away to the tabernacle to pray. As she prayed, she cried because she wanted a baby so much.

"Dear God, please give me a son. Let me have a baby, and I promise that I will lend him to you as long as he lives," Hannah prayed.

Hannah prayed so hard and cried so much that Eli noticed her. He prayed with her that God would give her the son she wanted. Hannah went away happily because now she believed that God would really answer her prayer.

That was exactly what happened. A little boy was born. Hannah called him Samuel.

1 Samuel 1

Samuel Goes to the Tabernacle

Hannah did not forget her promise to God. As soon as Samuel was old enough to leave home, Hannah and Elkanah took the boy Samuel to the tabernacle at Shiloh. Hannah led him to Eli the priest, and said, "The Lord has answered my prayer. Now I will lend my son to God as long as he lives."

Eli took Samuel and after they had prayed together, Hannah and Elkanah returned to their home in Ramah. Ramah was about eleven miles away from Shiloh.

Samuel grew to love the priest, Eli. He learned how to serve God in the tabernacle. Every year his parents came to see him. His mother, Hannah, always brought a new coat for him. They would go to the tabernacle to offer gifts to God. Eli would give them his blessing, "May the Lord send you other children to take the place of the boy you have lent him."

Then Hannah and Elkanah would return to their home. Two little girls and three boys were born to Hannah and her husband.

As each year passed, Samuel grew wiser. Everybody loved and respected him, especially Eli. Eli was a good man, but his sons were selfish and evil. They would not listen to their father. They did not worship God.

1 Samuel 2:11-36

God Speaks to Samuel

Samuel obeyed Eli and listened to his wisdom. One dark night in the tabernacle everything was very still. The old man, Eli, who was almost blind now, was sound asleep. The lamps were burning dimly. Young Samuel, too, was asleep.

Samuel heard a voice saying, "Samuel!"

Samuel called sleepily, "Here I am," and ran to see what Eli wanted.

"I didn't call," said Eli, "Go back to bed."

Samuel went back to bed again, but the voice called a second time, "Samuel! Samuel!" The boy went straight to Eli, "You did call me. Here I am," he said.

"I didn't call you, now go and lie down," said Eli.

As soon as Samuel had gone back to bed for the third time, the voice called to him, "Samuel! Samuel!"

Again he went to Eli saying, "But you did call me."

This time Eli knew that it must be God who was calling Samuel. He said: "Go back, and if He calls again, you must say, 'Speak to me, Lord. Your servant is listening!'"

Samuel went back to bed, and the voice called again, "Samuel! Samuel!"

"Speak to me, Lord. Your servant is listening," Samuel replied.

Then God talked to Samuel. "I am going to punish the sons of Eli for their wickedness. I have told Eli that his whole family must be punished."

Samuel was afraid to tell Eli what God had said, but Eli replied: "Tell me what happened. You must not keep anything back."

Samuel told Eli the whole story. Eli answered, "The Lord God does what he knows is right."

1 Samuel 3

Samuel the Judge

Samuel grew into a young man. He remembered all that God taught him. Soon the people learned that they could trust him and take his advice. They knew that he was wise and good. Everyone in Israel listened to his words. They knew that he would be their next judge and prophet chosen by God.

There was more and more fighting going on now. The Philistines were stealing land from the people of Israel. During one battle four thousand soldiers of Israel were killed. The people began to lose hope, but they had an idea.

"Let's send to Shiloh and get the ark of God's promise," they decided. "We will carry it before us into battle. The ark will save us from the Philistines."

A messenger went to Shiloh to the tabernacle and took the ark from its place. Eli's two sons were guarding the ark. They brought the ark back with them into the camp.

When the ark was carried into the camp, a loud cry went up from the Israelite soldiers. The shout was so loud that the Philistines were afraid. When they heard that the ark was with the Israelites, they believed that God had come down to fight against them.

The leaders of the Philistines called the soldiers together. "Be brave, Philistines, or we will be slaves of the Israelites."

The battle began again. The Philistines killed thirty thousand soldiers of Israel. When the Philistines slipped over to take the ark there was no one left to guard it.

A messenger ran back to Shiloh to give the message to Eli, "The Israelites have fled. Thousands of men have been killed. Your two sons have been killed. The Philistines have taken the ark."

Such news was too much for the old man. He fell down dead. Samuel became judge over all Israel. He said to the people: "Return to God. Do not worship other gods. If you serve him, God will free you from the Philistines."

Samuel traveled from city to city helping people solve their problems and giving his advice. The people had faith in him. They knew he was chosen by God to be a prophet and a judge.

1 Samuel 4; 7:3-17

Samuel Chooses a King

When Samuel was an old man, the people begged him to appoint a king to rule over them. At first he did not agree. He was afraid that a king would demand too much of his people. But God said to Samuel, "Listen to them. Find them a king."

In the village of Gibeah there was a young man named Saul. He was an Israelite and was taller than any other man in the land. His father, Kish, was a very rich man.

One day some of their donkeys had strayed away from the farm. Kish sent Saul and a servant to find the donkeys. They traveled three days without finding anyone who had seen them.

They were near the home of Samuel. The servant suggested: "There is a wise man in this town who knows many things. Let's go to him. Maybe he can tell us where to look."

It was a strange thing for Saul to visit Samuel. The day before, God had spoken to Samuel saying: "Tomorrow at this time, I will send a man from the tribe of Benjamin to you. Make him a king. He will save my people from the Philistines."

The strangers came into town just as Samuel was going out to the place of worship on the hill.

Samuel heard God saying, "This is the man I have chosen to rule over my people."

Samuel went to Saul and asked him to his house. That night Saul and the servant were Samuel's guests at supper. They slept in the finest rooms Samuel had to offer.

When it was morning, Samuel walked with Saul and the servant to the edge of town. Samuel asked Saul to send

the servant on ahead. "I want to speak with you alone," Samuel whispered.

When they were alone, Samuel filled a horn with some oil. He poured the oil on Saul's head, saying: "I anoint you in the name of the Lord. You will be king over all Israel and save us from the hands of our enemies."

Samuel called the people together at a place called Mizpah. There he told them the news.

"Here is the man chosen by God to be your king."

"God save the king!" the people shouted.

1 Samuel 8; 9; 10:1-24

David the Shepherd

David, the son of Jesse, was a shepherd boy. He was the youngest of eight brothers. David liked nothing better than to look after his father's sheep in the green hills outside of Bethlehem.

David loved all the beautiful things around him. He watched the seasons come and go each year. He loved to watch the birds and animals, the moon, the stars and sky. Nothing went unnoticed as David sat among the trees and flowers on the grassy slopes.

David loved the beauty so much that he would sit with his harp and sing songs about all the beautiful things around him. He sang of God's goodness to his people. One of the best known songs he ever sang was the 23rd Psalm.

The LORD is my shepherd; I shall not want.

He maketh me to lie down in green pastures:

He leadeth me beside the still waters.

He restoreth my soul:

He leadeth me in the paths of righteousness for His name's sake.

Yea, though I walk through the valley of the shadow of death,

I will fear no evil: for thou art with me;

thy rod and thy staff they comfort me.

Thou preparest a table before me in the presence of mine enemies:

thou anointest my head with oil;

my cup runneth over.

Surely goodness and mercy shall follow me all the days of my life:

and I will dwell in the house of the LORD for ever.

1 Samuel 16:11-12; Psalm 23

Samuel Anoints David

In those days God was not very pleased with Saul the king of Israel. God said to Samuel, the prophet: "Go to the house of Jesse. There you will find one of his sons. I have chosen this man to be king."

Samuel went to Bethlehem. There he asked Jesse to call his sons together. They were strong, good-looking young men. Seven of the brothers walked past Samuel. When Samuel saw Eliab, he thought this must be the one God had chosen. Eliab was tall and handsome.

God spoke to Samuel: "Samuel, do not look only at the face or height of a man. Look in his heart. It is what a man's heart is like that is the most important thing."

Then Samuel said to Jesse, "Have you any other sons?"

Jesse replied, "My youngest son is looking after my sheep out in the hills."

"Send for him," said Samuel.

When David came before Samuel, he heard God saying, "This is the one that I have chosen."

Samuel took a horn and filled it with oil. He poured the oil on the head of David in the presence of his brothers. From that time on David knew that God was with him in a special way. One day David would be the king of Israel.

1 Samuel 16:1-13

David the Singer

There was trouble in the king's house. Saul was sick in his mind. He lost his temper easily. He was worried and unhappy. He did not trust any of his friends.

Saul's servants tried to think of ways to help him. "Music might help the king," they suggested.

King Saul liked the idea. "Find a singer and bring him here," he ordered.

"I know someone who plays and sings," one of Saul's men answered. "It is David, the youngest son of Jesse of Bethlehem."

When David's father heard that the king needed his son, he sent David to him. David played his harp and sang. His music made the king feel much better. His songs of praise to God quieted the king.

After this, David played whenever the king felt ill. David's music helped King Saul recover from sickness many times.

1 Samuel 16:14-23

David and Goliath

For David, life was peaceful. But there was war in the land. The soldiers of Israel were at war with the Philistines.

David's three oldest brothers were now in the army of Saul. One day Jesse, David's father, sent David to see if his brothers were safe and well.

When David arrived, the two armies had set up their camps on opposite sides of the valley of Elah. Every day the Philistines sent out a giant called Goliath. Goliath was the champion warrior of the Philistines. He was nine feet tall. He carried a spear twice the size of any other soldier. It was so heavy that no man except Goliath could lift it. He wore a suit of armor and a helmet on his head.

David said to his brothers: "Who is this man who laughs at our army? Why doesn't someone go out and kill him?"

David went to King Saul. He begged Saul to let him go and fight the Philistine giant.

"But you are just a boy," replied Saul. "How can you fight such a big man? Goliath has been a warrior since he was a boy."

David said to him, "One day a lion and bear took a lamb from my father's flock. I killed the lion. Then I killed the bear. I was not hurt. I know God will be with me if I fight this giant.

When Saul saw that David was not afraid, he gave him his armor and sword. But David said, "I do not know how to fight in armor."

David went out and picked up five smooth stones and put them in his shepherd's bag. He took his slingshot in his hand and went out to meet Goliath.

When the Philistine saw that David was a boy, he said, "I will kill you and give your body to the birds of the air and the beasts of the fields."

David said bravely: "You have come to me with sword and spear. I come to you in the name of God. I will win. The world will know that God rules in Israel."

Goliath raised his sword, but David did not move. Then David took a step forward. He took out one of the stones from the leather bag and placed it in his sling. Goliath came toward him waving his sword in the air.

Suddenly David took aim. The stone from the slingshot flew through the air and hit Goliath on the head.

The giant fell to the ground. David ran up to him and picked up Goliath's own sword. He cut off the giant's head.

1 Samuel 17

David and Jonathan

After David the shepherd boy had killed Goliath, he became a soldier in King Saul's army. David was a hero now to all his people. But the one who loved him best was the king's son, Jonathan. Jonathan and David became the best of friends.

One day, Jonathan took off his robe and gave it to David as a sign of his friendship. He also gave David his sword and bow. From that day on they were as brothers.

King Saul was proud of David and loved him like a son. But when the people sang about David being a great soldier and about his victory over Goliath, Saul became jealous.

David still played his harp for the king. But the music did not help any more. One day, while David was playing for the king, Saul cried out: "I will kill you, David. I will pin you to the wall with my spear." He threw his spear at David. But God was with David and he avoided the spear.

Jonathan begged his father not to harm David, saying: "You must not do this to him. He has not sinned against you. Would you kill an innocent man without cause?"

Saul was ashamed of the things he had done. He remembered that it was David who had killed Goliath and saved Israel. He sent for David that they might live in peace.

1 Samuel 18; 19:1-7

David and Saul

Once again David and Jonathan and Saul lived together in peace. Saul was friendly to David.

Then Saul became jealous again. Once more he threw his spear at David. This time David ran away from Saul and never came back.

Jonathan was very disappointed when he heard what his father had done. He went to find David.

"What have I done? Why does the king want to kill me?" said David.

"You have done no wrong against my father. You will not die. He will not find you," Jonathan told David. "Whatever you ask from me, David, you know that I will do it for you."

"Tomorrow is the celebration of the new moon. It is my duty to sit at the king's table, but that would be dangerous. What should I do?" David asked.

"I will see if my father notices your empty seat. If he does, and is not upset, I will find you and let you know that it is safe to return. If I see that my father is still angry, I will warn you so you can escape," Jonathan told David.

"How will I know what your father says?" David wondered.

"I will come to this field with a young boy to practice with my bows and arrows. You hide behind the rocks. I will shoot three arrows into the air and then send the boy to find them. If I say, 'Look! The arrows are on this side of you,' you will know that it is safe to return."

"And if it is not safe," asked David, "what will you say?"

"I will say to the boy, 'Look! The arrows are beyond you.' That is your signal to go."

On the first and second days of the feast, Saul said nothing about David. On the third day he said, "Why is David not by my side, Jonathan?"

"He has gone to see his father in Bethlehem," replied Jonathan.

"Then he must be found and brought to me. This time he will die," said Saul angrily.

The next morning Jonathan went to the field where David was hiding. Jonathan shot his three arrows and called with a loud voice, "Look, the arrows are beyond you."

David knew that he must go quickly because his life was in danger. Jonathan told the young boy to walk on ahead. He did not want David to go without seeing him.

"Now go in peace," said Jonathan as David came out of hiding. Then they remembered their promise to one another. Sadly they said goodbye.

After time had passed, Saul took three thousand men to search for David. One night they were so close to each other that David, who was hiding in a cave, crept into the place where Saul was sleeping. From Saul's robe, David cut a piece of cloth.

When he had gone away from the place where Saul was sleeping, David shouted: "Saul, why do you think I want to hurt you? Why should I want to kill you?" David held up the piece of cloth. "You can see from this that I wish you no harm."

Saul was sorry he had treated David cruelly. He knew David could have killed him while he slept. "You are a better man than I am," Saul called to David. "You have done only good things to me. I have always treated you badly."

Though Saul said this, David could not believe that

he would mean it for long, so he went back into hiding.

David was right. Once again Saul began to hunt for him. When his camp was near, David went again to Saul's sleeping place. David took a famous spearsman called Abishai. They entered the camp together.

When Abishai saw the king asleep, he lifted his spear and said to David, "Let me kill Saul." But David said, "Let's take his water jug and his spear." They crept out of the camp and left Saul and his guard, Abner, asleep.

When they had gone to a hill, David called to Abner, "You deserve to die because you have not guarded Saul well."

"Is that your voice, David?" called Saul.

"It is," replied David, holding up the water jug to prove that they had just left the camp.

"I have done you wrong, David. I will never try to harm you again. Please come back to me," begged Saul.

David was not sure. Saul had broken his word so many times. David knew that Saul was often ill and did not know what he was doing. David decided not to go back.

Fighting broke out again between the Philistines and the Israelites. In a battle, Saul was wounded. His three sons were killed. One of them was Jonathan. Saul did not want to be killed by the Philistines so he fell on his own sword and killed himself.

Three days later a messenger told David that his friend Jonathan had been killed by the Philistines.

"And Saul?" asked David. "What has happened to him?"

"He is dead," said the messenger.

All day long David cried. He was very sad. He had loved both Jonathan and Saul.

Then David asked God what he should do. God said, "Go back to Israel to the land of Judah."

David obeyed. He went back to his country to become king of all Israel.

1 Samuel 18:1-16; 19:1-10; 20; 22:1-4; 23:14-18, 22-23; 24; 26; 28:3-6; 2 Samuel 1; 23:13-23; 1 Chronicles 10; 11:10-22; 12:1-2, 8, 15-18

David the King

David did not become king over a happy and peaceful nation. The people were fighting among themselves, and the Philistines were still their enemy. But David did exactly as God said and the Philistines were finally driven back into their own land.

For a long time the Ark of the Covenant had not been honored as it should have been. David decided that it should be brought to Mount Zion where a new tent of worship would be set up.

After this there was a time of peace for all of Israel. David lived quietly in his palace. God was worshiped in the tabernacle.

But David was not happy. It seemed wrong to him that he lived in a palace lined with cedar wood while the Ark of the Lord stood in a tent. When he told this to Nathan the prophet, Nathan said to him that he should go on with his plan to build a better place for the Ark.

But David never built a house for God. That night Nathan heard a message for the king. God told him: "David is a soldier, a fighting man. He is not to build a house for me. Go and tell David that. But also tell David that his son, Solomon, will be king and will build the Temple."

Now David began to make other plans. He went to work collecting materials so that someday Solomon might build a house beautiful enough for a place to worship God. He collected cedar wood, gold and silver, brass and iron. He stored away precious stones. David even chose the place where the Temple was to be built.

Then David called all his army, all his leaders, and all the princes of the land together. He told them: "Learn the laws of God. Obey his commandments so that you and your children and their children's children may enjoy this good land forever. My son, Solomon, will someday build a house for God where the ark of his promise might rest."

Then he handed to Solomon the plans for the Temple.

1 Chronicles 22; 28

A King Does Wrong

Even a king can do wrong. There came a time when David did something very wrong.

One evening as David was on the roof of his palace, he looked across to a nearby house. There he saw a beautiful woman. As soon as he saw her, he wanted her to be his wife. When he asked one of his servants, they told him that she was Bathsheba, the wife of one of his soldiers. The soldier's name was Uriah.

Then David had a terrible idea. If Bathsheba were a widow, she could be his wife. Somehow he must get rid of her husband.

David wrote a letter to Captain Joab. The letter said: "Send Uriah to the front line where the fighting is most dangerous. Then draw back the other soldiers so that he must fight the enemy alone."

Before long the king's messenger reported Uriah had been killed in battle. Now David could marry Bathsheba. But David's wrong displeased God. He sent Nathan the prophet to David to let him understand how great his sin was.

David hated the sin that made him feel far away from God. He fell to his knees and prayed:

"Have mercy on me, O God, in your kindness and love:

Blot out the evil I have done.

Wash me clean from my sin.

I know that I have sinned.

I have sinned against you.

Wash me now, and I shall be clean, whiter than snow.

Wash me clean. Give me back a heart that is pure.

You do not ask for sacrifice offerings. I could give them.

All you ask is a broken heart.

Lord, truly I am sorry. Do not despise me.

Do not turn away where I cannot find you.

Let me hear laughing and singing again.

Let me speak, and I will praise you,

Tell all the people of your mercy and your goodness,

For happy is the man whose sins are forgiven."

David knew that he was forgiven, but trouble was a part of David's life from that day on.

2 Samuel 11:1-3; 14:27; 12:1-13; Psalm 51; 32:1

Solomon the King

When Solomon became king, the kingdom of Israel extended from the river Euphrates to the border of Egypt. It went from the Mediterranean Sea in the west to the great desert in the east. There were not only Israelites living in the kingdom, but people belonging to the desert tribes as well.

To rule over a kingdom like that the young king needed to be very wise. He was only twenty years old.

A little while after he took over the kingdom, Solomon went to Gibeon to worship God. That night God spoke to Solomon in a dream and told him to ask for some special gift.

Solomon showed his real greatness. He said, "Give me an understanding heart to judge the people, that I may tell between good and bad."

Solomon did not ask for riches, but for wisdom. That pleased God. He gave Solomon what he wished for. God also gave Solomon riches and honor.

Solomon went back to Jerusalem. There he worshiped God again. It was not long before Solomon had the chance to show the wisdom God had given to him. Two women came to him with their tiny babies, but one baby was dead. Each woman said that the living baby belonged to her. They were angry with one another. They wanted the king to decide to which of them the living baby belonged.

King Solomon was wise. He called for a sword. Then he made a strange request. "Cut the living baby into two parts," he said, "so that each mother may have a part of the baby."

One mother cried: "O my king, don't do it, please! Let her have the baby. Do not kill the baby, please!"

The other mother said: "Cut the baby into two pieces. Then it won't be mine, but it won't be hers either."

"Give the baby to the mother who did not want it killed. It really belongs to her," King Solomon ordered.

Everyone in the palace was amazed at the clever way Solomon had found out which woman to whom the baby belonged.

King Solomon chose able leaders to help him govern the country. There were twelve main officers. Under them were many other officers. Part of their work was to see that the army was kept up to strength. Solomon had forty thousand horses for his chariots, and twelve thousand horsemen. There were many foot soldiers, and even men who rode on camels.

Solomon passed on his wisdom to the people. Not only the Israelites, but people from all the countries came to hear. The fame of Israel was greater than it had ever been before.

1 Kings 3; 4; 2 Chronicles 1

Solomon Builds the Temple

Solomon became the wealthiest king in the land. People came from everywhere to bring Solomon gifts and to listen to his wisdom. King Hiram of Tyre, who had been a friend of David's, also visited Solomon. He made a treaty of friendship with Solomon.

Solomon was getting ready to build the Temple in Jerusalem. His father, David, had planned for the Temple long ago.

Solomon obtained materials he needed for the Temple from King Hiram. Cedar trees and fir trees were chopped on the mountain and taken down to the sea. Then the wood floated in great rafts until it reached the place where it could be carried to Jerusalem.

The walls of the Temple were made of stone. All the blocks were shaped in the quarries. At the building place on Mount Moriah, they were fitted together. All the walls were lined with cedar wood, and the beams and roof were of cedar also. The walls were carved with figures of angels and palm trees and flowers. The inside of the sanctuary and the altar were covered with pure gold.

Inside stood the Ark of the Covenant which contained the two stone tablets on which Moses had written the Law God gave him on Mount Sinai. At the entrance to the Temple there were two carved pillars. This Temple took seven years to build. Thousands of people worked there.

When the great Temple was finished, Solomon gathered the people for worship. Solomon prayed with his people for God's guidance in knowing right from wrong. He prayed for God's protection against the enemies of the Israelites. He prayed for God's forgiveness when the people sinned, for Solomon knew that no person was perfect.

After the people had gone home, God told Solomon: "I have heard your prayer and I have blessed this house which you have built for me. If you will do all I have commanded you, then I will establish your royal throne over Israel forever."

But even Solomon, who was a very wise man, was not a perfect king. God had warned the Israelites not to marry anyone from a nation that worshiped idols. He knew that the people would be tempted to worship idols themselves. As the years passed, Solomon did not remember God's warning. Solomon himself was tempted to worship other gods.

God became very angry with Solomon and told him that as punishment for his sins, Solomon's enemies would inherit the land. But God did not forget the good things Solomon had done. God promised that some day Solomon's descendants would inherit the land again.

1 Kings 5 to 9; 2 Chronicles 3 to 7

Elisha and the Woman from Shunem

Elisha was a prophet. He showed the power of God to the people by healing the sick and performing miracles. Elisha traveled a lot.

In the town of Shunem, where Elisha sometimes stopped to rest, there lived a friendly woman and her husband. When they heard Elisha was coming by Shunem, they would ask him to stop for lunch. This happened so often that the woman and her husband built a small room where Elisha could stay whenever he wanted to.

Elisha wanted to reward this woman's kindness. But she said to him: "I live with my own people. I need nothing, thank you."

Elisha saw that the woman and her husband did not have a son. He said to her, "About this time next year you will have a baby boy of your own."

Elisha was right! The woman had a baby boy. The boy grew up. He was a healthy boy who worked with his father in the fields. One day the boy suddenly became very ill and died. His mother laid his body on the bed in Elisha's room.

Then she told her husband: "I must go find Elisha. Send for one of the servants. Bring me a donkey."

As fast as she could go, she went looking for Elisha. He saw her coming a long way off. When she reached Elisha, she threw herself down and took hold of his feet. She told him why she was so sad.

The woman would not go back without Elisha, so he went with her. As soon as he saw the boy, Elisha closed the door to the room. Then he prayed. He blew his own breath into the boy's lungs. He stretched his body on the boy's body. All the time he prayed.

Suddenly the boy sneezed. He opened his eyes.

Elisha called for the boy's mother. She was so happy she threw herself on the ground in front of Elisha. Then she picked up her boy. He was well again.

2 Kings 4:8-37

Amos

In the hill country of Israel a shepherd named Amos was hard at work taking care of his sheep. When the figs were ripe, Amos would harvest his crop.

Up there in the hills he heard God saying, "Amos, go and preach to my people in Israel."

Amos had never been a preacher. But he knew that he must obey an order that came from God. He went into the town of Bethel and began to preach.

At first the people liked the stranger who was dressed like a country shepherd. At first they liked the way he was talking.

" 'Three times, four times Syria has sinned, and I will not forget,' says the Lord. 'Fire will burn down the house of the king of Syria, and his people will be captured.

" 'Three times, four times the Philistines have sinned, and I will not forget. Fire will burn down the wall of Gaza, and the people will be destroyed.

" 'Three times, four times Tyre has sinned, and I will not forget. Fire will burn down the walls of Tyre, and the wall around the city.' "

The preacher went on. The enemies of Israel were to be punished for their sins. The people liked what Amos was saying.

Then Amos spoke again, " 'Three times, four times Israel has sinned. You have been my people, chosen from all the earth. But woe to you now for your sins! You cheat the poor. You break my laws.

" 'So now your punishment will come to you, and you will discover who your God is.' "

About that time the high priest of Bethel hurried up to Amos.

"Go away. Go back to Judah and preach there. Don't preach any more in Bethel."

The shepherd preacher said, "I am no prophet trained to preach. God sent me while I was still tending my sheep. He told me,

" 'Go and preach to my people in Israel. Their ways are evil.' "

"Hear the words of the Lord God," said the prophet Amos.

2 Kings 14:23-29; the book of Amos

Jonah

God loved everybody, even the people who lived in Nineveh. Nineveh was a large city in which many people lived.

The people of Nineveh were very busy selling and buying food, clothing, and other things. But they were not serving or worshiping the true God. They did not know or care about God's laws or commandments. Nineveh was called a wicked city.

God wanted to warn the people who lived in Nineveh. He spoke to a man named Jonah about the city.

God said: "Jonah, I want you to go to Nineveh and talk to the people there. Tell them that their city will be destroyed because of the wicked things they are doing."

Jonah knew about this city and he did not want to go because it was a wicked city. He did not want to leave his own home which was many miles from the city of Nineveh.

Jonah thought, and then he said: "I know what I will do. I will not go to Nineveh. I will go the other direction away from the city."

He went down to the seashore. There Jonah found a ship sailing to Tarshish, far away to the west. He said to the men on the ship, "I will pay my fare and go with you."

As they were on the ship, a great storm came upon the sea. The winds blew and the big waves covered the ship. The ship seemed as if it would break in pieces. All of the men were afraid.

"What shall we do?" they asked.

"Let us pray to our gods," said one. They began to pray but nothing happened. The storm grew worse.

The captain went to Jonah who was sleeping inside

the ship. He said, "Get up quickly and pray to your God. Maybe he can save us."

Jonah replied, "Throw me overboard into the sea and the storm will stop."

The men threw Jonah out into the waters and the sea became calm.

God had prepared a great fish in the sea to swallow Jonah. For three days, Jonah was in the fish. Then, the fish threw Jonah out on dry land.

God spoke to Jonah again, "Arise, Jonah, go to Nineveh and preach," said God. This time Jonah obeyed.

He said to the people, "In forty days this city will be destroyed if you do not stop your wicked ways!"

The king of the country said to the people: "Let us turn away from our wicked ways. Let us do what is right and be sorry for our sins."

The people of Nineveh did as the king asked. They turned away from their sins. They asked God to forgive them and spare their city. God loved these people even though they had been wicked. In answer to their prayer, God did not destroy the city.

the book of Jonah

Jerusalem is Captured

For many years the prophets of God had been telling the people that they must obey God. The prophets warned the people that God was not pleased when they were dishonest and when they did not worship him. The prophets warned that one day their country would be destroyed. But the people did not listen.

Then the terrible years began. King Nebuchadnezzar's soldiers attacked Jerusalem. They carried the king off to Babylon. They carried off the golden treasures from the Temple. The beautiful city of Jerusalem was ruined. The Temple was destroyed.

Along with the king, they carried away the princes and the soldiers. They took the artists and the skilled workers. They took the young men to grind their grain. They took the children to carry wood. They took away the leaders. The only people left behind were the poor and those who did not know how to work.

Far, far from Jerusalem the lonely people of Judah grew more homesick every day for their city. One day a messenger brought a letter to the people. The letter was from the prophet Jeremiah. He was giving them a message from God.

"Build yourselves homes. Settle down to live in Babylon. Plant gardens. Settle down with your families. Do not expect to come home for a long, long time—not for seventy years.

"Pray to me. I will be listening. When you search for me with all your hearts you will surely find me.

"I will bring you back together again. I will bring you home. For I have loved you with an everlasting love. With my love I will bring you home to me."

Jeremiah 28; 29; 30:10; 31

Daniel Refuses the King's Food

When Nebuchadnezzar, king of Babylon, captured Jerusalem, he took Jehoiakim, the king of Judah, prisoner. Jehoiakim was brought to Babylon along with his family and many of the young Israelites.

Nebuchadnezzar saw that some of the young Jewish boys were intelligent and handsome. He thought they would be worth educating. When they grew up they could serve him. He gave orders that they were to be taught the Chaldean language and to have special food and wine from his table.

Among those chosen were Daniel, whose name the king changed to Belshazzar, and three others who were Shadrach, Meshach, and Abed-nego. These boys who had been taught to believe in God felt strange in Babylon. There was no temple in which they might worship. But they made up their minds to follow God's laws and serve him faithfully.

The Jews had strict rules about what they could eat. They would not eat anything forbidden by the law. Daniel knew they could not eat the rich food from the king's table, especially the meat. He asked the servant in charge of food to give him and his friends vegetables and water instead.

The servant agreed to do so for ten days, but he was afraid. What would the king say if the boys starved?

At the end of the ten days he saw that the boys looked better and were healthier than the children who ate the rich food. He allowed David and the three other boys to go on eating the food they had chosen.

As time went on the boys learned. God helped them to learn new skills. At the end of three years the four

young men were brought before Nebuchadnezzar. When he talked with them, the king found them full of wisdom and understanding and wiser than his own wise men.

Daniel 1; 2 Kings 20:17-18

Daniel Interprets the King's Dream

King Nebuchadnezzar could not sleep at night. He had strange dreams. This happened every night, but when he awoke he could not remember the dream.

He sent for his wise men so that they might help him know what his dream meant. But because he could not tell them what the dream had been, they could not explain the dream.

Nebuchadnezzar was furious. He ordered that all the wise men of Babylon should be killed. By this time Daniel was one of the wise men. When he heard that he and his friends were to be killed, he went to the king. He asked for time to study about the mysterious dream.

The king agreed. Daniel and his three friends prayed to God for help. That night God told Daniel the secret. Daniel thanked God in these words: "Blessed be the name of God for ever and ever. He is wise and powerful. He sends the winter, the spring, summer, and the autumn. He takes kings away from their thrones and chooses kings. He sees the things that are hidden in darkness, for where he is there is always light. He teaches and he gives understanding. I thank the God of my fathers, for he has taught me secret things."

Daniel then went to the king and said: "There is a God in heaven who can tell secret things. He is telling

the king something that is going to happen. You saw, O king, a frightening image standing before you. Its head was made of gold. Its chest and arms were silver. Its sides were brass. Its legs were iron. Its feet were part iron and part clay. As you looked, a stone hit the image on its feet and broke them to pieces. The iron, the clay, the brass, the silver and the gold were all broken to pieces. The wind carried the pieces away. The stone that struck the image became a great mountain as big as the earth."

Then Daniel explained that the head of gold represented King Nebuchadnezzar. After him other kingdoms would follow, not quite so strong. But after these kingdoms, God would build a kingdom which could never be destroyed.

When the king heard this he fell on his face before Daniel. "Your God is greater than all the kings of earth." He gave Daniel gifts and made him governor over Babylon and chief wise man of the kingdom. The king allowed Daniel to have Shadrach, Meshach, and Abed-nego for his assistants.

Daniel 2

Daniel Interprets a Mysterious Message

Nebuchadnezzar's son was King Belshazzar. King Belshazzar was the last ruler of Babylon. He gave a feast and invited a thousand guests. He ordered the silver cups and bowls his father had captured from the Temple of Jerusalem to be brought for the feast. The guests drank from the silver cups and bowls that had been dedicated for worship in the Temple.

While the guests drank they praised their heathen idols made of gold and silver and wood and stone.

While they were feasting, they were frightened to see a man's hand writing on the wall of the room. The frightened king called for his wise men and for his magicians, but none of them could read the writing.

The queen, who had not been at the feast, told the king about Daniel. She said, "Your father, King Nebuchadnezzar, made him chief of the wise men."

So Daniel came to stand before the king. "You have used the cups and bowls from the Temple of God in your own feasting. You have praised idols which do not see or hear or know. You give no heed to God who gave you life. God has counted the years of your kingdom and ended it. You have been weighed on the scales, and you are too light. The Medes and the Persians will take your kingdom from you."

Belshazzar, who had promised a reward to any man who could explain the writing, ordered Daniel to be clothed in a purple robe and golden chain. He was to be the third ruler in the kingdom.

That very night the Persian armies attacked Babylon. King Belshazzar was killed and Darius the Mede became king.

Daniel 5

Daniel in the Lions' Den

King Darius the Mede changed the government of Babylon. He set up one hundred and twenty governors. Over them he appointed three presidents. One of the three, and head of them all, was Daniel.

This made the other presidents and the governors jealous. They began to find a way to get Daniel in trouble. They went to the king and asked him to make a law.

This law would put anyone in the lions' den who prayed to any god or man other than the king.

"Give the order, and sign it with your name, King Darius, and make it one of the laws of our people that cannot be changed."

King Darius nodded his head, and the law was made.

Daniel, although he knew of this new law, still prayed three times a day. In his room with the windows open toward Jerusalem, he gave thanks to God as he had always done. His enemies were quick to tell the king that Daniel was disobeying him.

When Darius knew what he had done in making the law he was very upset. He tried to think of some way in which Daniel could be saved, but the law of the land could not be changed.

The king gave the order that Daniel should be thrown to the lions. But the king said a curious thing to Daniel, "May the God you serve continually, deliver you."

Daniel was pushed into the lions' den. A big rock was used to close the door. The king sealed the door so that no one could move the rock and release Daniel.

Then the king went to his palace and spent a sleepless night. But in the lions' den Daniel was not afraid. The lions did not try to hurt him. He knew why he was safe. God looked after him.

The next morning the king hurried to the lions' den. "O Daniel," he cried, "has your God been able to save you from the lions?"

And Daniel replied: "O king, live forever. My God has shut the lions' mouths and they have not hurt me."

The king ordered Daniel out of the den. Then the king commanded that the men who had accused Daniel were to be thrown into the den of lions.

Darius ordered that Daniel's God should be worshiped everywhere in all the land.

Daniel 6

A Jewish Girl Becomes Queen

King Ahasuerus, king of all the Medes and Persians planned a great feast in his palace. The palace was so large that when the king gave a feast and invited all the princes of the land, they came and stayed for days. While the princes feasted in the king's palace, a special feast was held for the women in the palace of the queen, Queen Vashti.

On the seventh day of the feast, when the king and his guests had been celebrating in the king's palace, Ahasuerus sent for Vashti.

But the queen said no. She stayed with the women in her own rooms in the palace.

King Ahasuerus was furious. He felt he had been put to shame in front of his princes because his wife would not obey him. He called together his wise men to tell him what to do.

The wise men said that if the king did not so something, the wives of all the other princes would become disobedient. "Make a law," they said, "that Vashti is no longer queen and that someone else shall be queen instead. Then all the wives in this land will listen to their husbands."

The king sent letters to all the provinces commanding that the most beautiful girls be sent to the palace in Shushan so that he could choose his new queen.

In the town of Shushan there was a Jew named Mordecai. He brought his niece, Esther, to the palace.

"Tell no one that you are Jewish," Mordecai warned her.

Each day Mordecai walked past the court of the women to ask about Esther. Each day he and Esther waited to see whether she would be called to go before the king. Then the day came. Esther went to stand before the king. As soon as he saw her he loved her. He put the crown on her head, and all the court bowed before Queen Esther.

One day Mordecai heard two men talking together. They were planning to murder the king. Mordecai sent a message to Esther to tell her what was happening, and she warned the king.

Both of the men were put to death, and the whole story of how Mordecai saved the king's life was written in the book of history.

Esther 1; 2

Esther Saves Her People

King Ahasuerus made Haman in charge of all the princes in the kingdom. All the people in and around the palace bowed before Haman, but one man would not. That man was Mordecai. As a Jew, he would not bow before anyone except God.

Haman decided that Mordecai must be killed, and all the other Jews in the empire as well. He did not know that the queen was a Jew.

Haman went to the king. He promised the king that if he was allowed to put all the Jews to death, it would cost the king nothing.

Ahasuerus did not understand, but he trusted Haman. He gave permission to Haman to do what he wanted. Haman sent out a proclamation, sealed with the king's seal, that on the thirteenth day of the twelfth month, all the Jews should be killed.

When Mordecai heard this, he was terribly upset. He tore his clothes and put on sackcloth and rubbed ashes on his face.

The queen had not been told about Haman's proclamation, but her servants came to tell her about the way Mordecai was dressed. She sent clothes to him, but he would not have them.

When they were brought back, Esther asked a servant to find the reason for his sorrow. Mordecai sent the queen a copy of the order with this message: "Go to the king. Beg him to save our people."

Even the queen was not allowed to go into the king's court unless he sent for her. Queen Esther was afraid to go to the king. She let Mordecai know about this, but he sent back a message to her: "Do not think you can be safe,

even in the king's palace. If you do not speak now, God will find someone else to save his people, but you and your people will die. Who knows? Maybe you were sent to the kingdom for such a time as this."

When she received this message, Esther sent to Mordecai and asked him to get together all the Jews in Shushan to pray for her for three days. On the third day, she would go to the king. The king might have her killed, but she would not be afraid.

Three days later, Queen Esther dressed in her most beautiful clothes and went to the king. When she stood in the doorway, she looked so beautiful that the king fell in love with her all over again.

Esther smiled, "I wish to invite the king and Haman to a banquet." That was all she said.

When the feast came to an end, Ahasuerus again asked Esther what she wished. She answered that on the next day he and Haman should come to another banquet.

As Haman went out of the palace, he saw Mordecai. As usual Mordecai did not bow to Haman. Haman's wife told Haman to have carpenters build a place to have Mordecai hanged. "Get the king to have Mordecai hanged," she said to Haman.

That night King Ahasuerus could not sleep. He sent for one of his servants to read to him the story of his reign. When the reader came to the record of how Mordecai had saved his life, Ahasuerus realized that he had never rewarded Mordecai for what he had done. He sent for any of the princes who were in the court at the time. Haman was there waiting for a chance to talk to the king about hanging Mordecai.

The king asked Haman a question: "What should the king do for the man he wishes to honor?" Haman was sure the king was speaking about him.

"Let the royal robes be put on him. Let him be seated on the king's horse. Have the king's crown placed on his head. Proclaim to the people that this is the man the king wishes to honor," Haman told the king.

Then Haman received a shock. The king told him to go and do all this to Mordecai the Jew. Proud Haman obeyed the king.

Sadly Haman went home to tell the news to his wife.

While they were still talking, the king's messengers came to take him to the queen's banquet.

When the feast was over, King Ahasuerus asked Esther to tell him her request. Then she said: "I am asking for my life. I am asking for the lives of my people. We have been sold, my people and I, to be killed."

"Who dared to do this?" demanded the king.

Esther pointed to Haman. Haman was terrified. The king was so angry that he walked out into the garden. When he came back, one of the servants told him about the place Haman had built to hang Mordecai.

"Hang Haman on it," the king ordered.

Then the king gave orders to Mordecai: "Write this letter. Sign it with the king's name. Tell the Jews to rise up and fight against the people who attack them on the thirteenth day of the twelfth month."

Instead of a day of death and sorrow for the Jews, it became a day of great rejoicing.

Esther 4 to 9

The Rebuilding of the Temple

Soldiers had marched into the city of Jerusalem. They had torn down the beautiful Temple where God's people had worshiped. Homes had been destroyed. Many of the people had been taken to a faraway country as captives.

One day the king of that country, King Cyrus, heard that some of the people from Jerusalem wanted to return to their home country and rebuild the Temple in Jerusalem.

King Cyrus announced that those who wanted to return to Jerusalem might do so. A man named Zerubbabel was chosen to lead the people.

King Cyrus made another announcement that pleased the people who were returning to Jerusalem. He said:

"Even though some of you are not able to go back to Jerusalem, you may still have a part in rebuilding the Temple. You may give of your silver and gold or send food and some of your animals."

When the people reached Jerusalem, they had no place to live. The first thing they did was to build homes. Then they began work on the foundation of the Temple.

As the Temple was being repaired, there were men who gave of their money and jewels and animals and food to help the builders. There were builders and workmen who helped.

While the people were working on the Temple, some of the people who lived near Jerusalem caused so much trouble the workers had to stop their building.

A long time afterward two prophets told the people they should finish the Temple. Zerubbabel and the people started to work again to complete the Temple.

The enemies tried to stop them again, but they kept working. The builders had another problem. "We do not have enough materials to finish the Temple," they said.

After talking about the problem, the people decided to write a letter to King Cyrus. King Cyrus had died, however, and a new king, King Darius, was on the throne.

"See if you can find the records of King Cyrus," said King Darius.

The records were found. King Darius wrote to the people in Jerusalem: "Keep on working until the Temple is finished. We are sending all the materials you will need."

The people were glad to get the materials. They worked hard. At last the Temple was completed. The people came together to worship God.

For seven days the people stayed together and had a

feast of thanksgiving. They thanked God for his goodness to them.

Ezra 1:1 to 6:15

Nehemiah Rebuilds the Wall

The wall around Jerusalem had been torn down for many years. It was torn down when the Babylonians captured the city. At that time part of the people had been taken to Babylon as slaves. Still later Babylon had been captured by Persia.

Nehemiah, one of the Hebrews, was a servant to the King of Persia. It was his job to serve the king his food.

One day as Nehemiah was serving the king, the king asked: "Are you sick, Nehemiah? Why do you look so sad?"

"I am sad because Jerusalem, the city of my people, is still in ruins. The people are poor. Without a wall to keep the enemy tribes out of the city, the people cannot defend themselves." Nehemiah paused. Then he continued, "May I leave and go to Jerusalem to rebuild the wall?"

The king listened as Nehemiah described the ruined wall of the city. "How long will you be gone?" they asked. "When will you return?"

"As long as it takes to rebuild the wall," Nehemiah answered. "If it pleases the king, will you give me letters to the governors of the countries through which I must travel?

A letter to the keeper of your forest so that I can get wood would help."

The king wrote the letters Nehemiah requested. He also sent some of the soldiers from his army to protect Nehemiah.

When Nehemiah and the soldiers reached Jerusalem they rested for three days. Then one night Nehemiah took a few soldiers with him and rode around the city to inspect the wall. He saw stones from the broken wall lying in piles where they had fallen. He saw gates burned by fire.

The next morning Nehemiah told the rulers and the priests the reason for his visit to the city. "I have come to help you rebuild the wall and the city," he said. "God answered my prayer and the king has given us permission to use lumber from his forest."

The leaders said: "Let us rise up! Let us rebuild the wall."

The people began to work on the wall. They divided into groups. Each group took a part of the wall to rebuild. The priests made a new sheep gate. Others worked cutting stones.

The people were happy as they worked together. Even when their enemies jeered at them, they kept on working. When some of the enemy tribes planned to attack the workmen, Nehemiah gave his men swords to protect themselves. The men continued to work until once more the city of Jerusalem was surrounded by a strong wall.

Nehemiah 1; 2

The People Give Thanks

After the Temple and wall were rebuilt in Jerusalem, the people were very happy. Nehemiah called all the people to a great gathering. They met together and dedicated the

Temple to God. It would be a place where they could meet together to praise God and hear from his prophets.

For seven days the people stayed together and had a feast and thanked God for his goodness to them. They were so glad to be back in Jerusalem. They were happy to have a Temple where they could meet for worship.

When Ezra came to Jerusalem, he found the people doing some things that did not please God. But the people wanted to please God.

A great wooden pulpit was made and set up in the street. Ezra stood on the pulpit. In his hands was a copy of the Book of God's Law.

Sentence by sentence Ezra read the Law to the people. It took from early morning until the middle of the day. Some of the listeners wept when they heard the Law. They realized how often they had broken God's commandments.

On the next day Ezra met with the leaders so that he could carefully explain the Law to them. For seven days Ezra taught them.

The people promised that they would keep God's Law and love him. They would be careful to keep the Sabbath day. All the promises were written down and the leaders signed the promises in the name of the people.

Ezra and Nehemiah were good leaders. They helped their people be glad because God had blessed them. They had rebuilt the Temple and the wall. They had heard God's word read and explained. "We will always be happy," they said, "if we try to please God and obey his commandments."

Ezra 6:16-22; 10:1; Nehemiah 8

The New Testament

The Angel Gabriel Visits Mary

The land of Israel, or Judea as it was called, was the home of the Jews. When the story of the New Testament began, Israel was ruled by King Herod. Herod was appointed king by Emperor Augustus Caesar of Rome.

The Jews were very tired of being governed by the Romans. The Jews longed to be free. The prophets had said that one day God would send someone to deliver them from their enemies. This person would be called the Messiah.

The Jews hoped and prayed that the Messiah would soon come. They often thought and talked about what the Messiah would be like.

At this time, there lived in the city of Nazareth, in Galilee, a young woman called Mary. Mary was gentle and good, and she often prayed to God.

Soon Mary was to marry Joseph. Joseph was a carpenter who also lived in Nazareth. He was a kind, hardworking man.

One day when Mary was sitting alone, she was suddenly aware of someone else in the room. Mary was afraid.

Then a voice said: "Don't be afraid, Mary. I am Gabriel, the angel of the Lord. I have come to tell you that you are favored in the sight of God."

Mary did not understand what the angel meant. But she was not afraid any more.

"Listen," Gabriel said, "to you, Mary, will be born a son, and you will call his name Jesus. He will be great, and he will reign forever and forever.

Mary did not understand how all this could happen. But Gabriel told her: "The Holy Spirit will be with you,

and the Holy Child which shall be born to you will be the son of God."

When Mary heard these words, she said: "I am the servant of the Lord, and I will do all the things which are asked of me."

Then the angel went away. Mary decided to visit her cousin Elizabeth in the hill country of Judea.

Luke 1:26-39

Zacharias and Elizabeth

Elizabeth, Mary's cousin, was married to Zacharias. Zacharias was a priest and served at the Temple in Jerusalem. Elizabeth and Zacharias had no children. Because they were old, they did not expect to have any.

One day when Zacharias was busy in the Temple, an angel appeared to Zacharias. Zacharias was afraid, for he had never seen an angel before.

"Don't be afraid, Zacharias," the angel said. "Your prayers have been heard. You and Elizabeth will have a son. You will call him John."

Zacharias did not believe the message from God. The angel said: "Zacharias, because you do not believe, you will not be able to talk until the baby is born."

It was after this that Mary came to see Elizabeth. Mary was excited and anxious to tell Elizabeth her news.

When Mary saw Elizabeth, the Holy Spirit told Elizabeth the wonderful news that Mary was to be the mother of the Son of God. Elizabeth said to Mary, "Cousin, you are indeed blessed among women."

Then Elizabeth told Mary that she, too, was going to have a son whose name would be John. She told Mary that the angel said John would one day lead the people of Israel.

Mary was happy to hear Elizabeth's news. She and Elizabeth prayed together and thanked God for all that had happened.

Mary stayed with Elizabeth for about three months. It was a happy time for them and often they would talk of the great happiness that would be theirs when their sons were born.

Later, when Elizabeth's son was born, all her friends and family were happy and rejoiced with her. But Zacharias still could not speak.

When the baby was eight days old, Elizabeth and Zacharias were ready to give him a name and present him to God.

"Call him Zacharias after his father," some said.

"No, he is to be called John," Elizabeth said.

"There is no one in your family named John," the friends said.

Then Zacharias wrote on a tablet, "His name is John." Then Zacharias was able to speak, and he praised God.

This John became one of God's prophets, John the Baptist.

Luke 1:5-22,40-79

Mary and Joseph Travel to Bethlehem

Mary was engaged to marry Joseph. After telling Mary she was to be the mother of the Son of God, the angel also spoke to Joseph. The angel told Joseph that Mary was to have a child who would be God's Son.

After Mary's visit to Elizabeth, Mary and Joseph were married. Not long after they were married, the Roman Emperor, Augustus Caesar, wanted to make a list of all the Jewish people. The emperor wanted this list so he could collect taxes from everyone. This meant that the people would have to travel to their hometowns or to the hometowns of their fathers and place their names on the special lists there.

Mary and Joseph had to go to Bethlehem. It was a long journey. It was also a tiring journey for Mary, for soon her son would be born. Mary rode on a donkey, and Joseph walked beside her.

When Mary and Joseph got to Bethlehem, they found many people there already. There were so many people in Bethlehem that there was no room for Mary and Joseph at the inn. The only place that could be found for them was a stable.

Mary and Joseph spent the night in the stable. During that night, Mary's baby was born. Mary wrapped the baby warmly in swaddling clothes. Because there was no bed, Mary laid the baby on the sweet-smelling hay in the manger. And Mary named the baby Jesus, as the angel had said.

Luke 2:1-7

The Shepherds Hear the Good News

The night Jesus was born, a group of shepherds were in the fields near Bethlehem. The shepherds were looking after their sheep.

Suddenly, a great light shown around them, and an angel of the Lord stood by them. The shepherds fell down on their knees with their faces to the ground because they were afraid.

The angel spoke to them: "Do not be afraid! I have come to bring you good tidings of great joy, for unto you and all people is born tonight a Saviour who is Christ the Lord. And this shall be a sign unto you. You shall find the baby wrapped in swaddling clothes and lying in a manger."

Suddenly there appeared with the angel of the Lord a great number of angels. The angels sang together: "Glory to God in the highest, peace, good-will to men." Then the angels disappeared, and the night was dark again.

The shepherds looked at one another. Then they said to one another, "Come, let us go to Bethlehem and see the baby. So the shepherds went from their fields into Bethlehem. There they found Mary and Joseph and Baby Jesus in the stable.

When the shepherds left Joseph and Mary, they went out and told everyone what they had seen, and the people were very, very glad. Then the shepherds went back to their sheep. They thanked God for all that they had seen and heard.

Luke 2:8-17

King Herod and the Wise Men

After Jesus was born in Bethlehem, wise men from far away in the east came to Jerusalem. They had been led by a star which moved ahead of them. They knew the star would lead them to the one who was born King of the Jews.

When they got to Jerusalem, they did not know where to go to find the baby, so they went to the court of Herod the King. "Where is the one who is born King of the Jews?" the wise men asked Herod. "We have come to worship him. We saw his star in the east."

These words upset Herod very much, and he gathered the chief priests and learned men together. "Where is this child and who is he?" King Herod asked these men.

"In Bethlehem of Judea," the chief priests told King Herod. "The prophets wrote that the Christ would be born there."

Herod was angry when he heard these things. He was afraid the baby born in Bethlehem would take his throne away from him. But Herod had a plan. He pretended he, too, wanted to worship the child. He told the wise men what the chief priests had said. Then he said: "Go and search well for the child. When you have found him, come and tell me, and I will go and worship him too."

As the wise men started on their way to Bethlehem, they saw the star again. They followed it until it stopped over a house. They went in and found Mary and Joseph and the young child.

The wise men kneeled down and worshipped Jesus. Then they gave him gifts of gold and frankincense and myrrh.

After the wise men left Jesus, they did not go back

to Herod. While they slept, they had a dream telling them not to go. So the wise men went home a different way.

Matthew 2:1-12

Mary, Joseph, and Jesus Go to Egypt

After the wise men left, Joseph had a dream, also. In the dream an angel came to Joseph and said: "Get up and take the Child and his mother and flee to Egypt. Go as quickly as you can. Stay there until I tell you to return. King Herod is looking for Jesus. Herod wants to kill Jesus.

So Joseph got up, and he woke Mary. Then he got the donkey ready for the trip to Egypt. Mary got Jesus ready. While it was still dark, Mary and Joseph, and Jesus started to Egypt.

Not long after they had gone, King Herod's soldiers arrived in Bethlehem. They did not find Jesus because Joseph had been warned by God.

The journey to Egypt was very long and hot. Mary and Joseph and Jesus were very tired. But at last they reached Egypt. How happy they were. They had escaped from Herod. Now they were safe.

After they got to Egypt, Mary and Joseph set up their new home there. They waited for the day when God would tell them to go back to their home.

Matthew 2:13-16

Return to Nazareth

Mary and Joseph and Jesus lived in Egypt as long as King Herod lived. But after some time King Herod died.

After the cruel king's death, the angel came to Joseph again. This time the angel told Joseph to go back to his own country.

"King Herod, who wanted to kill Jesus, is dead," the angel said. "It is safe to go back to your country."

So Joseph and Mary got ready to go back to their own country. Soon they were ready, and Joseph, Mary, and Jesus started on the long trip back home. They did not go back to Bethlehem, for another wicked king had taken Herod's place. An angel came once more and warned them instead to go to the part of the country called Galilee.

So Joseph took Mary and Jesus to the town of Nazareth. In Nazareth, Jesus grew up. Nazareth was not a big town, and its people were not very highly thought of in the rest of the country. But Jesus lived there.

Matthew 2:19-23

Jesus Goes to the Temple

Like all other faithful people in the land, Joseph and Mary went to Jerusalem once every year for the Feast of the Passover. The Feast of the Passover lasted a whole week. When Jesus was twelve years old, Mary and Joseph took him with them. He was now old enough to take part in the festival.

This was an important occasion for a Jewish boy. At twelve years old, he could become a "son of the Law." From then on he would be held responsible for his own deeds like any grown man.

It was a long trip to Jerusalem. On the way the family was joined by other people from different parts of the country. Finally, there was a large group of people traveling along together. It was a dangerous trip because there were so many robbers in the hills. Being a large group together made them safe from the robbers.

From the Mount of Olives just outside Jerusalem, Mary and Joseph and Jesus and the others could see the city for the first time. Across the valley they could see at once the white marble buildings and the golden roof of the Temple.

Luke 2:41-42

Jesus Talks to the Doctors

When the Feast of the Passover had ended, Mary and Joseph joined the group of people from Galilee. They started on their trip home to Nazareth.

There was such a crowd that they did not notice that Jesus was not with them. At the end of the day they could not find Jesus. They hunted for him. They asked their relatives and friends. But no one had seen Jesus. Mary and Joseph looked everywhere. But Jesus was not to be found. So Mary and Joseph started back to Jerusalem.

On the third day, they got to the Temple. To their surprise, they found Jesus sitting in one of the courts with the teachers and the doctors. He was listening to them and asking them questions.

A crowd of people were listening to Jesus and the teachers and doctors. The people were surprised at how much Jesus knew. They were surprised at the wise questions Jesus was asking.

But Mary was upset that her kind and loving son, who had always been so thoughtful, should have worried them so. She said: "Son, why have you treated us like this? Joseph and I have been so worried. We've looked everywhere for you."

"Why have you looked for me?" Jesus said. "Did you not know that I must be about my Father's business?"

Mary and Joseph did not understand what Jesus meant by that. But Jesus was telling them that his first work, his great work, would always be to serve God.

From the Temple, Jesus went back to Nazareth with Mary and Joseph. He obeyed them as a good son should.

Luke 2:43-51

Jesus Calls His Disciples

When Jesus went to preach in Galilee, he needed many helpers because there was so much to do. So Jesus chose twelve men who became known as his disciples. Each one was going to help Jesus in his work with the people.

One day as Jesus walked by the Sea of Galilee, he saw two fishermen. They were brothers, and their names were Simon Peter and Andrew. Jesus called to them, and they left their fishing nets and followed Jesus.

Jesus saw two other brothers who were fishermen. Their names were James and John. Jesus called to these two brothers and they also left their fishing nets and went with Jesus.

Later Jesus saw a man named Philip. Philip became one of Jesus' disciples. One of Philip's friends, Bartholomew (sometimes called Nathanael) also became one of Jesus' disciples.

One day Jesus saw a man who collected taxes from the people. He was Matthew, a tax collector. Jesus said, "Matthew, follow me." And Matthew left what he was doing and became one of Jesus' disciples.

Besides these men, Jesus chose five others to be his disciples. They were: Thomas, Thaddeus, James the son of Alphaeus, Simon, and Judas Iscariot.

They all came from different types of homes. Some were educated men and some were just ordinary working men. Some were fishermen. Each of them wanted to serve Jesus so much that he was ready to give up his life work to help Jesus.

Matthew 4:18-22; 9:9; Mark 1:16-20; 3:16-19; John 1:43-51

Jesus Teaching

Jesus climbed a little way up the side of a mountain near the Sea of Galilee. He sat down there and called his disciples to come sit close to him. The other people who had followed sat down on the ground nearby.

Jesus talked to the people. He told them how people must live who belong to the kingdom of God. He explained to them the rules of the kingdom. One of the things Jesus said was: "Blessed are the peacemakers: for they shall be called the children of God."

Jesus also told the people that day some important things about the way to treat their enemies. He said they were to love their enemies. They were to do good to people who hated them, and they were to pray for people who mistreated them.

Jesus told the people many other things that day about how to love God and other people.

Matthew 5; Luke 6

The Good Samaritan

One of the best-known stories or parables that Jesus told is about the good Samaritan.

One day a man tried to trick Jesus into giving the wrong answer to a question. The man asked what he must do to have everlasting life.

"What do you think you must do?" asked Jesus. "What is written in the commandments?"

The man answered: "You must love the Lord your God with all your heart, and with all your soul, and with all your strength, and with all your mind; and you must love your neighbor as yourself."

"That is the right answer," said Jesus. "Do this and you will have everlasting life."

But the man knew very well that he had not loved the Lord his God with all his heart. Neither had he loved his neighbor as himself. He wanted to find an excuse for himself, so he asked, "But who is my neighbor?"

Then Jesus told this story: A man was on his way from Jerusalem to Jericho when he fell into the hands of thieves. They beat him and tore off his clothes and left him half dead by the roadside.

By chance a priest came down the road. When he saw

the wounded man, he passed by on the other side.

Later a second man came along. He, too, only looked at the hopeless man and passed by on the other side of the road.

Then a Samaritan came along the same road. When he got to the place where the poor man was lying, he stopped. When he saw how hurt the man was, the Samaritan poured oil and wine on his wounds and bandaged them. Then he put the man on his donkey and took him to an inn and looked after him.

The next morning, when he left, the Samaritan gave the innkeeper two silver coins. "Take care of the poor fellow," he said. "If there is any more to pay, I will pay you when I return."

"Now," asked Jesus, "which of these three men do you think was a neighbor to the man who fell among thieves?"

"The man who took pity on him," the man answered who had asked Jesus the question.

"Then go and do the same," Jesus said.

Luke 10:25-37

The Parable of the Talents

Jesus told another story about a man who went on a long journey. Before he left, he called his servants in. He told the servants he was putting them in charge of his property. He gave twelve hundred and fifty pounds (ten talents) to one servant. To another servant he gave five hundred pounds, or five talents. And to the third servant he gave two hundred and fifty pounds (one talent).

The servant who had been given the most money began trading with it. He made a profit of twelve hundred and fifty pounds. The man who had been given five hundred pounds made a profit of five hundred pounds. But the man who had been given two hundred and fifty pounds went and dug a hole in the ground and buried the money in it.

Some months afterward the master came home. He asked his servants what they had done with his money. The man who had been given twelve hundred and fifty pounds handed it back to his master with another twelve hundred and fifty pounds. "Master," he said, "you gave me twelve hundred and fifty pounds, and I have made a profit of another twelve hundred and fifty pounds."

The master was very pleased. "Well done!" he said. "You have proved yourself a good and faithful servant. Because you have done a small job well, I will give you charge over many things."

Then the servant who had been given five hundred pounds came forward. "Master," he said, "you gave me five hundred pounds and I have made a profit of another five hundred pounds."

"Well done!" said his master. "You have proved yourself a good and faithful servant. Because you have done a small job well, I will give you authority over much."

The servant who had been given two hundred and fifty pounds came up. "Master," he said, "I know you are a hard and keen businessman. I know you make profits where you do not sow. Because of this, I was afraid to risk your money. I dug a hole in the ground and hid the money there. Here you are. It's safe."

"You lazy servant," said his master. "You know very well that I expected you to work to earn profits for me. You should have put my money in the bank, then when I came home, I would have got my money back plus the

interest. Take the two hundred and fifty pounds and give it to the servant who has the most money."

Jesus was saying that God expects us to do our best and not to be lazy and waste our time.

Matthew 25:14-29

A Foolish Rich Man

"Be careful of greediness," Jesus said. "Life is not really made up of the things you own."

Then Jesus told another parable, a story, to explain what he meant.

There was a rich man whose land produced much crops. When he harvested the crops, his storerooms were all filled.

The rich man thought to himself: "What shall I do? I don't have enough room to store my crops. I will pull down my barns, my storerooms, and build bigger ones. Then I will have room for all my grain and all my goods. Then I will say to myself: You have enough grain and goods to last for years. Sit back and take it easy. Eat, drink, and be merry."

But God said to that man: "Fool! This night your life will be taken from you. Who then will get all you have saved for the future?"

Jesus said, "This is what happens to the man who stores up worldly goods but does not worry about the riches of God."

Luke 12:16-21

The Parable of the Sower

One parable Jesus told was about a sower and his seed.

"There was a man," said Jesus, "who went out to sow seeds in the ground. On his way home some seed dropped by the wayside. The birds came down at once and ate up the scattered seed. The rest of the seed was stepped on and pushed in the ground.

"Then the sower dropped some seed onto rocky ground. As soon as it grew, it quickly died, for there was no water to keep it alive. It dried up.

"The seed that the sower dropped onto thorny ground fell among thornbushes. When it grew, the thornbushes grew too. They choked the seed.

"Now the seed which fell onto good ground grew into healthy plants. These plants had fine fruit on them because they had been well sown. You must listen to these things that I tell you," Jesus added.

The disciples did not understand. "What does this story mean?" they asked.

"The seed is the word of God," Jesus said. "The wayside is like people who hear what God has said to them but do not take any notice. The rocky ground is like people who are happy to hear God's word but they have no roots when trouble comes along.

Thorny ground is like people who love riches and are always looking for pleasure. These people never do anything perfectly. They only think of themselves.

"The good soil," said Jesus, "is like people who are honest. When they hear God's word, they remember it, and do what God says."

Matthew 13:3-8; Mark 4:1-9; Luke 8:4-15

The Servant and the Money

Jesus told His disciples a story about a king who sent for his servants one day. He told the servants they must pay him all they owed him.

One of the servants was upset. He owed very much indeed, more than he could possibly pay. And now the king threatened to take all his possessions and sell him and his wife and children as slaves.

How he pleaded with the king! "Give me time, and I will pay you all," he said. The king felt so sorry for him, that he forgave him the whole debt, as big as it was.

But then the man went out and found one of his fellow-servants who owed him some money. It was only a very small amount. But he took the man by the throat and demanded that he should pay at once.

This poor servant begged for time, but the first servant would not help him at all. He had the poor man put in prison.

Other servants had seen this, and they went at once to tell the king. When the king heard, he was very angry. He called the first servant to him. "You wicked man," he said. "You begged me to forgive you the very great debt you owed me, and I did. But now you refuse to have mercy on your fellow servant for a very much smaller debt. To prison you go at once. And you will stay there until you have paid every penny."

Then Jesus said, "This is how my heavenly Father will treat you. too, if you are not willing to forgive other people."

Matthew 18:23-35

The Prodigal Son

Jesus told a parable we call the story of the prodigal son.

"A certain rich man," said Jesus, "had two sons, whom he loved very much. One day, the younger son came to his father. He said, 'Father, please give me my share of the things which you have saved for me, that will one day be mine. I would rather have them now, while I am still young, then I can enjoy myself.'

"So the father gave the son his share of his riches and said no more about it. Not many days after he had done this, the son packed his belongings and left his father's house.

"The elder brother did not ask his father for his share of the riches. Instead he stayed at home and helped his father to look after his house and land.

"Meanwhile the younger son traveled to a country far away and settled down among strangers.

"At first everything went well for him. He was rich and had many friends. He did not work, but wasted all his money and spent everything that he had on amusing himself. He never stopped to think about his family who had been so good to him.

"It was not long before he had spent all his money. There was nothing left, and his friends left him because he was no longer rich. Then a famine came upon the land. This meant that there was no food. The young son was alone and without money.

"He soon found that he had to look for work, but there was little he was able to do. At last a man offered him a job looking after pigs. He did not like this job, but he had no choice for he was starving. Even with the job, he earned so little that he still went hungry. He became

so unhappy that he began to think how foolish he had been. He wondered how his family were getting on. While he was so miserable, they had plenty to eat, for their table was always full of good food. There was more than enough for his parents and his brother, and the servants were well fed and cared for, too.

"At last the son could bear it no longer, and he decided to walk back to his own country. It was very far, and he was tired and hungry.

"One day when his father was standing outside his house, he saw in the distance a tired, limping young man, dressed in rags. Although the man was so far off, the father knew it was his son at once. He ran out to welcome him.

"The tired young man almost fell in his father's arms. He was tired and ashamed of what he had done. He said: 'Father, forgive me. I have sinned against God and no longer deserve to be called your son.'

"But his father brought him into the house and gave him his robe, put a ring on his finger, and shoes on his feet. 'Bring the fatted calf and let us prepare a great feast,' he said joyfully, 'for my son who was lost is found.'

"At first the elder brother was angry because his father paid so much attention to his brother. But his father said, 'You have always been a good son to me. All that I have is yours, but we must forgive your brother because he is really sorry. Surely we must rejoice because he has come home.'"

Luke 15:11-32

Jesus Preaches From a Boat

Jesus often preached beside the Sea of Galilee. He walked along the seashore, and often he talked to the fishermen there who were mending their nets.

Like all ports and seaside places, it was always busy. That is why Jesus liked to preach there. People from many different countries came there.

Often Jesus would speak to the people on the beach. Sometimes he would stand in a boat and talk to the people gathered on the shore.

Sometimes a great crowd of people came there to hear Jesus. One day there was such a crowd that they pushed against Jesus. With such a crowd, not many could hear what Jesus said. So Jesus got in a boat. He rowed a little way from the shore. That way more people could hear him.

On this day, Jesus taught the people many things. Some of the things he told the people were in stories. When Jesus told a story, it had a special meaning. This kind of story is called a parable.

Based on Matthew 13:1-2; Mark 4:1-2

Jesus and the Children

Whenever Jesus went into the countryside, children followed him. Jesus loved to sit with the children. Wherever he was, they would run and sit on his knee or get as close as they could to him. The children knew that Jesus loved them very much.

Jesus liked to watch the children play games together. No matter how tired Jesus was, he liked to have the children at his side. Sometimes he told them stories which they liked to hear.

One day when he was speaking to a crowd of people, some mothers came with their children. They wanted the children to see Jesus and be blessed by him.

The disciples thought Jesus was too busy to be bothered by the children. They told the mothers to take the children home.

When Jesus saw his disciples sending the children away, he said: "Let the children come to me. Do not stop them. They are the kind of people God wants for his kingdom. They are his children."

Mark 10:13-16; Luke 18:15-17

The Rich Young Ruler

One day as the disciples were walking along with Jesus, a rich young man who was passing by came up to Jesus.

The rich man asked Jesus: "What must I do to live forever in thy kingdom?"

"You must keep all of God's commandments," Jesus told the rich young ruler. Then Jesus went on to say: "You must not lie. You must not steal. You must always love your parents. You must help your neighbors."

The rich young man answered Jesus: "But I have done all of these things. I have done them since I was a child. What more can I do?" he asked.

"Just one more thing," said Jesus. "Will you give up everything that you own? Will you give it all to the poor and come and help me in my work?" Jesus asked.

The rich young ruler looked ashamed. He knew that although he tried to do all that he could, it was not enough. He liked to be rich. He liked the things he

owned. He was not ready to give away all that he had.

So he turned and went on his way. He was sad because he felt he had failed God, yet he could not find it in his heart to do anything about it.

Matthew 19:16-22; Mark 10:17-22; Luke 18:18-23

Jesus' Miracles

Jesus had been invited to a wedding feast in the village of Cana in Galilee. He and some of his disciples went. Jesus' mother, Mary, was there too.

The feast was a happy one until they ran out of wine. How ashamed the hosts must have felt when there was not enough food and drink for everyone.

But Mary had an idea. She went to Jesus and told him that there was no more wine. Then she told the servants to do whatever Jesus told them to.

Jesus asked the servants to fill the waterpots with clean water. And the servants did. Then he told them to dip out some of the water and take it to the master of ceremonies.

When this man tasted it, he was surprised. He had been told there was no more wine. Now they brought him this. And this was the best wine he had tasted so far.

The master of ceremonies went to the bridegroom to ask about the wine. "At all feasts," he said to the bridegroom, "they serve the best wine first and keep the poor wine until last. But you have saved the best wine until the last."

This was the first miracle done by Jesus. Later he would do many more.

John 2:1-11

Calming the Storm

One evening when the sun was setting, the disciples got into a boat to row across the Sea of Galilee to Capernaum. Jesus stayed on the mountainside by himself.

As the disciples started to row across the lake, a storm came up. The wind became strong and the waves were rough. The storm got worse, and the disciples could not row against the fierce waves. The wind tossed their boat about on the water. Soon it was dark.

When Jesus saw their trouble, he quickly went down to the seashore. He walked straight into the stormy water.

When the disciples saw a man walking toward them in the stormy water, they were very afraid. But Jesus called out to them: "It is I. Be not afraid."

The moment Jesus stepped into the boat, the winds stopped and the sea became calm.

Matthew 14:22-32; Mark 6:45-51; John 6:16-21

The Boy and His Lunch

One day the disciples had been with Jesus at a place in the countryside. The whole place was packed with people who wanted to be near Jesus. They wanted to hear his words. They brought their sick relatives for him to heal.

Even when he had finished preaching to them, they would not go away. Jesus was afraid they would be hungry. He said to the disciples: "We must feed them, for there is no place here for them to eat."

The disciples asked Jesus: "Do you want us to go and buy two hundred pennies worth of bread?"

"What food do you have?" Jesus asked.

"Five loaves of bread and two fish," the disciples said. "That is all we can find. They belong to a boy in the crowd."

"Give them to me," Jesus said. The boy handed his basket of food to Jesus. "Tell the people to sit down on the grass," Jesus said.

Then Jesus took the bread and gave thanks to God for it. Then he broke the bread and gave it to the disciples to give to the people. Then he did the same thing with the fish. And there was more than enough food to feed the five thousand people sitting on the ground.

When the people saw this, they knew that Jesus was sent from heaven, and they believed in him.

Matthew 14:13-21; Mark 6:31-44; Luke 9:10-17; John 6:1-14

Jesus Healing

As Jesus went about Galilee preaching, great crowds followed him. One day when he was near Capernaum, he stayed at the house of Simon Peter.

While Jesus was there, Simon Peter's mother-in-law became sick with a dangerous fever. When Jesus heard this, he at once went in to her and lifted her up. He touched her with his hands and at once the hot fever left her body. She was well again. She was so well that she got up from her bed at once.

When the people heard this wonderful thing, the news spread quickly. Soon great numbers of people were outside the door. They brought with them sick friends who were suffering from all kinds of terrible illnesses. Jesus was very tired, but he came out to the people. He began to heal them and to comfort them.

Matthew 8:14-16; Mark 2:28-34; Luke 4:37-41

Jesus Heals the Blind Man

One day, while Jesus was walking down one of the streets in Jerusalem, he saw a man who had been blind from birth.

The disciples asked Jesus about this man. "Master," they said, "who sinned, this man or his parents, that he should be born blind?"

Jesus' answer must have surprised them. "It was neither this man nor his parents," Jesus said. "This has happened so that the works of God might be shown in him."

When Jesus had said this, he spat on the ground. Then he made clay with the saliva. He touched the blind man's eyes with the clay. Then Jesus told the blind man to go and wash in the pool of Siloam.

Friends of the man came and led him away to the pool. When he came back, he could see as well as anyone.

All the people who had known this man when he was blind were surprised. "How could this have happened?" they asked. "How were your eyes opened?"

"A man named Jesus made clay," the man said. "He put the clay on my eyes and told me to go and wash in the pool of Siloam. I did what he said and now I can see."

Other people asked the man questions. Not all of them believed what he said. Some thought Jesus was a sinner. The leaders of the synagogue put the man out of the synagogue because of what he said.

When Jesus heard this, he asked the man, "Do you believe in the Son of God?"

"Who is he, that I might believe?" the man asked.

Jesus said, "He is talking to you right now."

Then the man said, "Lord, I believe."

At another time Jesus and his disciples went to Jericho. A great crowd of people were there to welcome him. Near the gate was a poor blind beggar.

When the blind man heard Jesus was near, he cried out in a loud voice, "Jesus, have mercy on me."

As the people brought the blind beggar to Jesus, the man said, "Lord, let me receive my sight."

"Your faith in me has cured you," Jesus said. "Receive your sight now."

At once the poor beggar could see. He was very happy as he looked at Jesus. He praised God with all his heart.

Mark 10:46-52; John 9:1-41

The Man Through the Roof

Once when Jesus was in Capernaum, so many people went to see him that there was not room for them all in the house where he was. While Jesus preached inside, crowds gathered outside the door, listening for his voice.

Then four men came. They were carrying a man who was paralyzed. They tried to get through the crowd to see Jesus. But no one would let them through.

The four men carried the sick man up to the roof. Then they tied ropes to the corner of the straw mattress on which he lay. The roof was made of tiles, and the men took some of the tiles away until there was a hole in the roof. When the hole was big enough, they let the sick man down through the hole.

Jesus looked up. He saw the sick man, and he saw the four friends looking down from the roof. He knew how much faith these men must have.

Jesus said to the sick man, "My son, your sins are forgiven."

This did not please some of the people who thought that Jesus was saying what only God had any right to say. "Only God can forgive sins," they thought.

Jesus knew what they were thinking even though they did not say the words out loud. "Which is easier to say?" he asked, "Your sins are forgiven, or to say 'Rise, take up your bed and walk'?"

The people who doubted did not answer, and Jesus went on. "But so that you may know that the Son of man has power on earth to forgive sins," he turned to the sick man and said, "I say to you, rise, and take up your bed and go home."

The man at once got up from the bed and stood up

straight and tall. The people were amazed as he rolled up his bed and hurried away to meet his friends.

There was gladness and joy and the people praised God. "We have never seen anything like this," they said.

Matthew 9:1-8; Mark 2:3-12; Luke 5:18-26

Jesus and the Leper

One day Jesus was passing by a certain village. He heard that there were ten men who had a terrible disease called leprosy. Whoever had this disease had to stay away from their families. Usually the lepers gathered together in a group outside the town and kept away from all their friends.

When the lepers saw Jesus coming toward them, they called out to him, "Jesus, have mercy on us."

Jesus was not afraid of their disease. He came up to them and said: "Go back to your priests, and by the time you get there you will be cured."

They started back to their homes at once. As they went, they were cured of their terrible disease, just as Jesus had promised.

One of the men, when he knew what had happened, turned around. He ran back to where Jesus was and fell down in front of Jesus. The man Jesus healed praised God and thanked Jesus for making him well.

Jesus turned to his disciples and said: "Were there not ten men? Where are the other nine?"

Then he said to the man: "Rise, and go your way. Your faith has made you well."

Luke 17:11-19

Jesus Praying

Jesus prayed often. Sometimes he went out on the mountainside by himself to pray. Sometimes he prayed late at night.

One day when Jesus had finished praying, one of his disciples said to him, "Lord, teach us to pray."

Jesus said to these friends: "When you pray, say:

Our Father which art in heaven,
Hallowed be thy name.
Thy kingdom come.
Thy will be done in earth,
as it is in heaven.
Give us this day our daily bread.
And forgive us our debts,
as we forgive our debtors.
And lead us not into temptation,
but deliver us from evil:
For thine is the kingdom, and the power,
and the glory, for ever, Amen.

At other times Jesus taught his disciples more about prayer.

Matthew 6:9-13

"This Is My Son"

While Jesus was traveling about teaching and healing, he made a special point of explaining to his disciples who he was and what he had come to do. One time Jesus called Peter and James and John to go with him to a quiet place at the top of a high mountain.

While Jesus was praying there on the mountain, Peter and James and John fell asleep. All at once they awoke and saw Jesus there by them. But Jesus was changed. He looked different. His clothes had turned to a shining white. They were whiter than anyone on earth could make them.

As Peter and James and John looked at Jesus, they saw two other men. Standing by Jesus were Elijah and Moses. They were talking to Jesus. After a while, Elijah and Moses seemed to be saying good-bye to Jesus. Peter called to Jesus then: "Master, it is good for us to be here. Let us make three tabernacles. We'll make one for you, one for Elijah, and one for Moses." But Peter did not really understand what was happening.

As Peter spoke, a cloud began to form over the mountaintop. The disciples were afraid. Then they heard a voice out of the cloud: "This is my Son, my chosen One. Listen to him."

When Peter and James and John looked again, Jesus was alone.

Matthew 17:1-8; Mark 9:2-8; Luke 9:28-36

The Triumphal Entry

Jesus and his disciples were on their way to Jerusalem for the Passover Feast. They came to the town of Bethany where they spent the night.

Jesus sent two of the disciples on an errand. He asked them to go into the next village. As soon as they came to the village, they would find a donkey and her colt tied up. They must untie the donkey and the colt and bring them to Jesus. If anyone stopped the disciples and asked what they were doing, they were to say that the Lord needed the donkey.

(All of this was done to make come true what the prophet Zechariah had said a long time before.)

The disciples brought the donkey to Jesus. Then they spread their cloaks on the back of the donkey, and Jesus got on.

As Jesus began slowly to move along the road into Jerusalem, crowds of people watched. Some spread their cloaks in the way. Others cut down palm branches and spread them on the road in front of Jesus.

As Jesus went by, the people shouted his praises:

"Hosanna to the Son of David:
Blessed is he who comes in the name of the Lord;
Hosanna in the highest."

When Jesus and those with him got to Jerusalem, all the people who saw and heard them were puzzled. "Who is this?" they asked.

"This is the prophet Jesus, from Galilee," the crowd with Jesus answered.

Matthew 21:1-11; Mark 11:1-11; Luke 19:28-40; John 12:12-19

Getting Ready for The Last Supper

The disciples asked Jesus: "Where do you want us to get ready to eat the Passover meal?"

Jesus answered them in a strange way. He said: "Go into the city and you will find a certain man there. Tell him that the Master says that his time is at hand. Tell him that the Master wants to keep the Passover with his disciples at his house. The man will understand."

Peter and John went into the city. As they walked along a street, they saw a man carrying a jar of water. (This was how Jesus said Peter and John would know the man.)

Peter and John followed the man to his room. When he went in, they asked him where the guest room was. They told the man that the Master wanted to eat the Passover there. When the man showed the room to Peter and John, they began to get the room ready for the Passover. All the food had been prepared. Now Peter and John waited for Jesus and the other disciples.

Matthew 26:12-18; Mark 14:12-16; Luke 22:7-13

The Crucifixion

Not long after Jesus and his disciples ate the Passover supper together, one of the disciples, Judas Iscariot betrayed Jesus to the priests and rulers of the Temple who were against Jesus. Jesus knew this would happen. In fact, he had told the disciples it would.

Jesus had told the disciples that he would leave them, that he would be put to death, that he was going back to Heaven to live with the Father. He also had told them the Father would send another helper to them, the Holy Spirit. But the disciples did not fully understand what He was saying.

After Jesus and the disciples left the room where they ate the Passover supper, they went toward the Mount of Olives and into the Garden of Gethsemane. Jesus asked the disciples to wait and he went farther into the garden to pray. Judas had left earlier by himself. After some time Jesus came back to the disciples who were waiting. As he talked to them, Judas came up. He was with some of the rulers from the Temple.

Judas, when he saw Jesus, ran ahead and kissed Jesus. This was the signal to identify Jesus. The soldiers who were there came to take Jesus. Peter at first wanted to fight, but Jesus told him no. Jesus agreed to go with them.

The soldiers took Jesus to Caiaphas, the high priest. There he had a trial. The priests and rulers agreed he was guilty of claiming to be God's Son when they did not believe he was. They agreed he should be put to death.

Under the Roman law, however, the Jewish rulers could not sentence a person to death. So the Jewish rulers took Jesus to Pilate, the Roman governor. Pilate could find no reason for putting Jesus to death, but after a long time, he told the Jewish rulers to do what they wanted to with Jesus.

The soldiers made fun of Jesus. They called him a king. They put a crown of thorns on his head. They gave him a dry weed for a scepter, and they put a scarlet robe on him.

Then the soldiers took Jesus away to a hill called Golgotha where he would be put to death on a cross. He was to be crucified.

Even while Jesus was on the cross, people came to know he was the Son of God. One of these was a thief who was being crucified on a cross next to Jesus. Another was a Roman soldier who was watching.

When Jesus died, the thick curtain in the Temple tore apart. This curtain separated the altar where only the high priest could go from the rest of the Temple where

others could go. With Jesus' death, everyone could go to God in worship without a priest to help him.

Friends of Jesus took his body from the cross and buried him in a tomb. But Jesus had told his disciples he would not stay dead. On the third day, some women went to the tomb. They found it empty. Jesus had risen.

After that Jesus came several times to his disciples and followers. He still had more to tell them before he went back to Heaven to be with the Father.

One of the most important things he told them was to go to all nations and preach to the people and to tell them about the Father, the Son, and the Holy Ghost. Jesus also promised to be with them always.

Matthew 26:36 to 28?20; Mark 14:26 to 16:20; Luke 22:39 to 24:53; John 18 to 25

Peter and John at Gate Beautiful

In the early days of the church the apostles had wonderful powers given to them by God. One afternoon at about three o'clock, the time for evening service, Peter and John went up to the temple. When they got to the gate of the temple called the Beautiful Gate, they found sitting there a beggar who had been lame from birth.

As Peter and John came by, he asked them for a gift to help him. Peter and John stopped and looked at him. Peter said to him: "Look at us."

The man thought that they were going to give him some money. But Peter said: "I have no silver or gold, but what I have I give to you. In the name of Jesus Christ of Nazareth, stand up and walk." Then he took the man by the right hand, and lifted him up. The man's feet

and ankle bones were strong in that very moment. The man jumped up, and he walked with Peter and John into the temple. And he praised God.

All of the people there saw him. They were amazed, because they knew he was the man who had sat at the temple gate. They knew he could not walk. They crowded around to see. And then Peter began to tell the people about Jesus.

Acts 3:1-12

Saul on the Road to Damascus

Saul was angry with the Christians. He wanted them to be persecuted. He wanted them to be persecuted in all places where there were Jewish people living and where the Christians had come. He went to the high priest and asked for a letter of authority. He wanted to go to Damascus to the synagogues there to arrest any Christians and bring them as prisoners to Jerusalem.

These letters were given to Saul by the high priest, and Saul soon left for Damascus. While he was on his way to Damascus, Saul had time to think about Christ and His gospel.

At last Saul came near to Damascus. The long journey was nearly over. Then suddenly a light that was brighter than the sun shone from heaven around Saul. Saul fell to the ground. Then he heard a voice saying to him: "Saul, Saul, why do you persecute me?" Saul answered: "Who art Thou, Lord?" Then the voice spoke again: "I am Jesus whom you are persecuting. It is hard

for you to fight against me. Go now into Damascus and you will be told there what you must do."

The men who were traveling with Saul stood there. They did not know what to say. They heard a voice but they did not see anyone. When Saul got up from the ground, he could not see. Others had to lead him by the hand until they came to Damascus. For three days Saul could not see.

In Damascus there lived a disciple of Jesus named Ananias. In a dream God told him to go see Saul. Ananias had heard of Saul. He was afraid Saul's visit was a trick. But God told Ananias that he had work for Saul to do.

So Ananias found Saul. He laid his hands on Saul and said: "Brother Saul, Jesus, who appeared to you while you were coming to Damascus, has sent me to you so that you may see again.

Saul stayed with the disciples in Damascus for a long time. Every day he went into the synagogues and told the people about Jesus. He told them Jesus was God's Son. The people who heard him were surprised. They knew that he had hated the Christians. But now he said Jesus is God's Son.

Saul, who became known as Paul, spent the rest of his life as a missionary. He traveled to many cities and towns, telling people about Jesus.

The rest of the New Testament tells about Paul and other Christians in the early church.

Acts 9:1-22

BIBLE QUIZ

THE OLD TESTAMENT

GOD MAKES THE WORLD

Who made the world?
What things did God place in the world to make it more beautiful?

THE FIRST MAN AND WOMAN

What were the names of the first man and woman?
Where did they live?
How did God make Eve?
From what tree did God forbid Adam and Eve to eat fruit?

ADAM AND EVE DISOBEY GOD

Who tricked Eve into eating the forbidden fruit?
How did God punish Adam and Eve?
How did God punish the serpent?

THE FIRST TWO BROTHERS

What kind of work did Cain do?
What kind of work did Abel do?
What did Cain do to his brother?

NOAH BUILDS AN ARK

Why was God willing to save the lives of Noah and his family?
What did God tell Noah to take into the ark with him?

THE FLOOD

How long did it rain?
What did the dove bring back to the ark?

THE RAINBOW PROMISE

What is the first thing Noah did when he left the ark?
Why did God send the rainbow?

ABRAM AND LOT MAKE A CHOICE

What promise did God make to Abram?
What kind of land did Abram have left after sharing with Lot?

ABRAHAM, SARAH, AND ISAAC

What was the promise God made to Abraham
What did the name Isaac mean?

ABRAHAM'S TEST

How did Abraham prove that he trusted God?
What did God provide for Abraham to sacrifice instead of Isaac?

A WIFE FOR ISAAC

What did the servant ask God to do to help him find the right wife for Isaac?
Why did Rebekah's father allow his daughter to leave to become Isaac's wife?

JOSEPH AND THE BEAUTIFUL COAT

What special gift did Jacob give to Joseph?
What did Joseph's brothers do to him because of their jealousy?

JOSEPH THE SLAVE

What happened to Joseph in Egypt?
What did Potiphar do to Joseph?

JOSEPH IN PRISON

What did the dreams of the butler and the baker mean?
What was the meaning of Pharaoh's dream?
What suggestion did Joseph make to Pharaoh?
What was Joseph's reward?

JOSEPH THE RULER

What did Joseph do after Pharaoh made him in charge of all the land of Egypt?

JOSEPH AND HIS BROTHERS

What did Joseph do to test his brothers?
Why was Jacob upset when his sons returned with wheat from Egypt?

BENJAMIN'S CUP

What did Joseph's servants put in Benjamin's sack of grain?
What did Joseph tell his brothers to do to escape the famine in their own land?

JACOB BLESSES JOSEPH'S SONS

Why did Jacob and his family stop at Beersheba?
What did God say to Jacob about going to live in Egypt?

MOSES IN A BASKET BOAT

What terrible thing did the Pharaoh decide to do?
How did Amran save her son's life?
Who found the baby, and what did she do with him?

MOSES RUNS AWAY FROM THE PALACE

Why did Moses have to run away into the land of Midian?

GOD CALLS MOSES

What strange thing happened to Moses in the desert?

What did God promise to do for Moses and the children of Israel?

MOSES LEADS HIS PEOPLE TO FREEDOM

What did Pharaoh do when Moses and Aaron went to see him?

What special warning did Moses and Aaron give to Pharaoh?

What was the last and worst plague?

How were the Israelites to prevent the final plague from hurting them too?

Who was to guide the Israelites on their journey?

THE TEN COMMANDMENTS

What was the most important thing that happened at Mount Sinai?

What were the Ten Commandments God gave to Moses?

THE BATTLE OF JERICHO

What happened to the Jordan River when the Israelites started to cross?

What did God tell Joshua?

How did the Israelites take the city of Jericho?

JOSHUA REMEMBERS CALEB

What did Caleb want from Joshua?

GIDEON

Why did God tell Gideon that he had too many soldiers?

How did Gideon decide which soldiers to keep and which to send home?

A STRONG FIGHTER

What was the good news the angel gave to Manoah's wife?

What was the riddle Samson asked?

SAMSON LOSES HIS STRENGTH

What was the secret of Samson's strength?

Who got the credit for Samson's capture?

Why did Samson have to be led to the pillars of the temple?

NAOMI LEAVES BETHLEHEM

Why did Elimelech and Naomi go to live in Moab?

What did Ruth do and what did she say to Naomi?

RUTH GATHERS GRAIN

How did Ruth get food for herself and Naomi?

RUTH AND BOAZ

What wonderful thing happened to Ruth?

HANNAH PRAYS FOR A SON

What did Hannah want more than anything?

What promise did Hannah make to God if he would answer her prayer?

SAMUEL GOES TO THE TABERNACLE

How was Samuel different from Eli's sons?

GOD SPEAKS TO SAMUEL

What message did God give to Samuel?

SAMUEL THE JUDGE

What did the people of Israel decide to do to help the army?

What did Samuel tell the Israelites to do?

SAMUEL CHOOSES A KING

How did Samuel know that Saul was the man to be king?

DAVID THE SHEPHERD

What do we call the songs that David wrote and sang?

SAMUEL ANOINTS DAVID

How did God tell Samuel that Eliab was not the one to be king?

What did God tell Samuel when David came before him?

DAVID THE SINGER

Why was David brought to King Saul's house?

DAVID AND GOLIATH

Why did David not use Saul's armor and sword to fight Goliath?

What weapon did David choose?

What did David say to Goliath?

DAVID AND JONATHAN

What did Jonathan give David as a sign of friendship?

Why was Saul angry with David?

DAVID AND SAUL

How did Jonathan save David's life?

What did David do to Saul rather than kill him?

What did David and Abishai take from Saul's camp?

What did David do when he heard that Saul was dead?

DAVID THE KING

Why was David unhappy in his palace lined with cedar wood?

What was the message God gave to the prophet Nathan?

A KING DOES WRONG

What wrong did David do?
What did David do when Nathan told him God was not pleased?

SOLOMON THE KING

How old was Solomon when he became king?
How did Solomon show real greatness?

SOLOMON BUILDS THE TEMPLE

What did Solomon do when the Temple was finished?
What was the warning God gave to Solomon?

ELISHA AND THE WOMAN FROM SHUNEM

What special favor did the woman at Shunem and her husband do for Elisha?
What did Elisha do to return the favor?

AMOS

What message did Amos give to the people of Bethel?

JONAH

Why was Jonah afraid to go to Ninevah?
Did Jonah obey God the next time he told him to do something?

JERUSALEM IS CAPTURED

What did Jeremiah say in his letter to the prisoners in Babylon?

DANIEL REFUSES THE KING'S FOOD

Why would the prisoners not eat the food from the king's table?

DANIEL INTERPRETS THE KING'S DREAM

How was Daniel able to tell the king his dream and its meaning?
What reward came to Daniel and his friends?

DANIEL INTERPRETS A MYSTERIOUS MESSAGE

What did Belshazzer see that frightened him?
What did Daniel tell the king about the words on the wall?

DANIEL IN THE LIONS' DEN

What office did Darius give to Daniel?
How did Daniel break the king's law?
How was Daniel punished?
Why couldn't the king sleep?
How was Daniel saved from the lions?

A JEWISH GIRL BECOMES QUEEN

How did Queen Vashti make King Ahasuerus angry?
What was the plot Mordecai overheard?

ESTHER SAVES HER PEOPLE

Who refused to bow before Haman?
What did Esther ask Mordecai and all the Jews to do for her?
How did the king find out about Haman's order that the Jews were to be killed?

THE REBUILDING OF THE TEMPLE

What message did King Darius send to the people in Jerusalem?

NEHEMIAH REBUILDS THE WALL

Who helped Nehemiah rebuild the wall?

THE PEOPLE GIVE THANKS

What did some of the people do when Ezra read from the Book of God's law?
What promise did the people make?

THE NEW TESTAMENT

THE ANGEL GABRIEL VISITS MARY

What was the message the angel gave to Mary?

ZACHARIAS AND ELIZABETH

What did the angel tell Zacharias in the Temple?

MARY AND JOSEPH TRAVEL TO BETHLEHEM

Why did Joseph and Mary go to Bethlehem?
Why did Joseph and Mary have to spend the night in a stable?

THE SHEPHERDS HEAR THE GOOD NEWS

What was the wonderful news the angel brought to the shepherds?
What did the shepherds do after they had seen Jesus?

KING HEROD AND THE WISE MEN

How did the wise men find the baby?
Why did the wise men not go to Herod after finding Jesus?

MARY, JOSEPH, AND JESUS GO TO EGYPT

Why did King Herod's soldiers not find Jesus?

RETURN TO NAZARETH

Why did Mary, Joseph, and Jesus go to Nazareth instead of Bethlehem?

JESUS GOES TO THE TEMPLE

Why did Mary and Joseph go to Jerusalem every year?

JESUS TALKS TO THE DOCTORS

Why did Mary and Joseph have to go back to Jerusalem?
Where did they find Jesus?

JESUS CALLS HIS DISCIPLES

What were the helpers Jesus chose called?

JESUS TEACHING

How did Jesus teach people to treat their enemies?

THE GOOD SAMARITAN

Why did Jesus tell the story of the good Samaritan?

THE PARABLE OF THE TALENTS

What did Jesus help us know by telling the story about the man who went on a long journey?

A FOOLISH RICH MAN

What did Jesus teach about greediness?

THE PARABLE OF THE SOWER

What lesson was Jesus teaching when he told the story of the sower?

THE SERVANT AND THE MONEY

What story did Jesus tell to teach about forgiveness?

THE PRODIGAL SON

When did the Prodigal Son decide to go home?
How did the father greet his son who had been away?

JESUS PREACHES FROM A BOAT

What are the stories which Jesus told sometimes called?

JESUS AND THE CHILDREN

What did Jesus tell his disciples about children?

THE RICH YOUNG RULER

What did Jesus tell the rich man to do to live forever?

JESUS' MIRACLES

What was the first miracle Jesus did?

CALMING THE STORM

What did Jesus say to the frightened disciples during the storm?

THE BOY AND HIS LUNCH

How was a little boy's lunch made to feed so many people?

JESUS HEALING

What happened when the people heard about Jesus healing Peter's mother-in-law?

JESUS HEALS THE BLIND MAN

What did the blind man say when his friends asked him how his eyes were opened?
What did the poor blind beggar do when he could see?

THE MAN THROUGH THE ROOF

What did Jesus say to the man who had been lowered through the roof?

JESUS AND THE LEPER

How many of the ten lepers thanked Jesus for making them well?

JESUS PRAYING

How did Jesus teach his disciples to pray?

"THIS IS MY SON"

What did Peter, James, and John do when Jesus told them to keep watch?

THE TRIUMPHAL ENTRY

What did the people say as Jesus went by?

GETTING READING FOR THE LAST SUPPER

How did Peter and John find a place to have the Last Supper?

THE CRUCIFIXION

What happened when Jesus died?
What happened on the third day after Jesus was buried?

PETER AND JOHN AT GATE BEAUTIFUL

What miracle did Peter and John perform?
To whom did Peter give credit for what he and John had done?

SAUL ON THE ROAD TO DAMASCUS

Why was Saul on his way to Damascus?
What special job did God have for Saul to do?

Hymns for Young Folks

A special collection of hymns, Christmas carols and patriotic songs which are the favorites of Christian young people.

INDEX

Tell Me the Story of Jesus

Fanny J. Crosby   Jno. R. Sweney

1. Tell me the sto-ry of Je-sus, Write on my heart ev-'ry word;
2. Fast-ing a-lone in the des-ert, Tell of the days that are past.
3. Tell of the cross where they nailed Him, Writh-ing in an-guish and pain;

CHO.—*Tell me the sto-ry of Je-sus, Write on my heart ev-'ry word;*

Tell me the sto-ry most pre-cious, Sweet-est that ev-er was heard.
How for our sins He was tempt-ed, Yet was tri-um-phant at last.
Tell of the grave where they laid Him, Tell how He liv-eth a-gain.

Tell me the sto-ry most pre-cious, Sweet-est that ev-er was heard.

Tell how the an-gels, in cho-rus, Sang as they welcomed His birth,
Tell of the years of His la-bor, Tell of the sor-row He bore,
Love in that sto-ry so ten-der, Clear-er than ev-er I see:

"Glo-ry to God in the high-est! Peace and good ti-dings to earth."
He was de-spised and af-flict-ed, Home-less, re-ject-ed and poor.
Stay, let me weep while you whis-per, Love paid the ran-som for me.

Wonderful Words of Life

1. Sing them o - ver a - gain to me, Won - der - ful words of life;
2. Christ, the bless - ed One, gives to all Won - der - ful words of life;
3. Sweet - ly ech - o the gos - pel call, Won - der - ful words of life;

Let me more of their beau - ty see, Won - der - ful words of life.
Sin - ner, list to the lov - ing call, Won - der - ful words of life.
Of - fer par - don and peace to all, Won - der - ful words of life.

Words of life and beau - ty Teach me faith and du - ty:
All so free - ly giv - en, Woo - ing us to heav - en:
Je - sus, on - ly Sav - iour, Sanc - ti - fy for - ev - er:

REFRAIN

Beau - ti - ful words, won - der - ful words, Won - der - ful words of life;

Beau - ti - ful words, won - der - ful words, Won - der - ful words of life.

Standing on the Promises

R. K. C.

R. KELSO CARTER

1. Stand-ing on the prom-is-es of Christ my King, Thro' e-ter-nal
2. Stand-ing on the prom-is-es that can-not fail, When the howl-ing
3. Stand-ing on the prom-is-es I now can see Per-fect, pres-ent
4. Stand-ing on the prom-is-es of Christ the Lord, Bound to Him e-
5. Stand-ing on the prom-is-es I can-not fall, Lis-t'ning ev-'ry

a-ges let His prais-es ring; Glo-ry in the highest I will shout and sing,
storms of doubt and fear as-sail, By the liv-ing Word of God I shall pre-vail,
cleansing in the blood for me; Standing in the lib-er-ty where Christ makes free,
ter-nal-ly by love's strong cord, O-ver-com-ing dai-ly with the Spir-it's sword,
mo-ment to the Spir-it's call, Rest-ing in my Sav-ior, as my all in all,

Chorus

Standing on the prom-is-es of God. Stand - ing, stand - ing,
Standing on the promises, Standing on the promises,

Stand-ing on the prom-is-es of God my Sav-ior; Stand - ing,
Standing on the prom-is-es.

stand - ing, I'm stand-ing on the prom-is-es of God.
Stand-ing on the prom-is-es,

Tell Me the Old, Old Story

Kate Hankey

W. H. Doane

1. Tell me the Old, Old Sto-ry, Of un-seen things a-bove, Of Je-sus
2. Tell me the sto-ry slow-ly, That I may take it in— That won-der-
3. Tell me the sto-ry soft-ly, With ear-nest tones and grave; Re-mem-ber
4. Tell me the same old sto-ry, When you have cause to fear That this world's

and His glo-ry, Of Je-sus and His love; Tell me the sto-ry
ful re-demp-tion, God's rem-e-dy for sin; Tell me the sto-ry
I'm the sin-ner Whom Je-sus came to save; Tell me the sto-ry
emp-ty glo-ry Is cost-ing me too dear; Yes, and when that world's

sim-ply, As to a lit-tle child, For I am weak and wea-ry,
oft-en, For I for-get so soon, The "ear-ly dew" of morn-ing
al-ways, If you would real-ly be, In an-y time of troub-le,
glo-ry is dawn-ing on my soul, Tell me the Old, Old Sto-ry:

Chorus

And help-less and de-filed.
Has passed a-way at noon. Tell me the Old, Old Sto-ry, Tell me the
A com-fort-er to me.
"Christ Je-sus makes thee whole."

Old, Old Sto-ry, Tell me the Old, Old Sto-ry Of Je-sus and His love.

Bringing in the Sheaves

Knowles Shaw

George A. Minor

1. Sow - ing in the morn - ing, sow-ing seeds of kind - ness, Sow-ing in the
2. Sow - ing in the sun - shine, sow-ing in the shad - ows, Fear-ing nei - ther
3. Go - ing forth with weep-ing, sow-ing for the Mas - ter, Tho' the loss sus-

noon - tide and the dew - y eve; Wait - ing for the har - vest,
clouds nor win - ter's chill - ing breeze; By and by the har - vest,
tained our spir - it oft - en grieves; When our weep-ing's o - ver,

and the time of reap-ing, shall come re - joic - ing, bring-ing in the sheaves.
and the la - bor end - ed, We shall come re - joic - ing, bring-ing in the sheaves.
He will bid us wel-come, We shall come re - joic - ing, bring-ing in the sheaves.

CHORUS

Bring-ing in the sheaves, bring-ing in the sheaves, We shall come re-joic-
Bring-ing in the sheaves, bring-ing in the sheaves, We shall come re-joic-

1. ing, bring - ing in the sheaves;
2. ing, bring-ing in the sheaves.

A Charge to Keep I Have

CHARLES WESLEY

LOWELL MASON

1. A charge to keep I have— A God to glo-ri-fy,
2. To serve the pres-ent age, My call-ing to ful-fill —
3. Arm me with jeal-ous care, As in Thy sight to live;

Who gave His Son my soul to save And fit it for the sky.
O may it all my powers en-gage To do my Mas-ter's will!
And O Thy serv-ant, Lord, pre-pare A strict ac-count to give!

Stand Up for Jesus

G. DUFFIELD

G. J. WEBB

1. Stand up, stand up for Je-sus, Ye sol-diers of the cross, Lift high His
2. Stand up, stand up for Je-sus, The trump-et call o-bey; Forth to the
3. Stand up, stand up for Je-sus, Stand in His strength a-lone; The arm of

roy-al ban-ner, It must not suf-fer loss; From vic-t'ry un-to vic-t'ry, His
might-y con-flict, In this His glorious day. "Ye that are men now serve Him," A-
flesh will fail you—Ye dare not trust your own; Put on the gos-pel ar-mor, Each

ar-my shall He lead, Till ev'ry foe is vanquished And Christ is Lord in-deed.
gainst unnumbered foes; Let courage rise with danger, And strength to strength oppose.
piece put on with prayer, Where du-ty calls, or dan-ger, Be nev-er want-ing there.

Savior, Like a Shepherd Lead Us

Anonymous

WILLIAM B. BRADBURY

1. Sav - ior, like a shep-herd lead us, Much we need Thy ten-der care;
2. We are Thine; do Thou be - friend us, Be the Guardian of our way;
3. Thou hast promised to re - ceive us, Poor and sin-ful though we be;
4. Ear - ly let us seek Thy fa - vor; Ear - ly let us do Thy will;

In Thy pleas-ant pas-tures feed us, For our use Thy folds pre-pare:
Keep Thy flock, from sin de - fend us, Seek us when we go a-stray:
Thou hast mer - cy to re - lieve us, Grace to cleanse, and pow'r to free:
Bless - ed Lord and on - ly Sav - ior, With Thy love our bos-oms fill:

Bless-ed Je - sus, Bless-ed Je - sus, Thou hast bought us, Thine we are;
Bless-ed Je - sus, Bless-ed Je - sus, Hear Thy chil-dren when they pray;
Bless-ed Je - sus, Bless-ed Je - sus, Ear - ly let us turn to Thee;
Bless-ed Je - sus, Bless-ed Je - sus, Thou hast loved us, love us still;

Bless-ed Je - sus, Bless-ed Je - sus, Thou hast bought us, Thine we are.
Bless-ed Je - sus, Bless-ed Je - sus, Hear Thy chil-dren when they pray.
Bless-ed Je - sus, Bless-ed Je - sus, Ear - ly let us turn to Thee.
Bless-ed Je - sus, Bless-ed Je - sus, Thou hast loved us, love us still.

Onward, Christian Soldiers

SABINE BARING-GOULD

ARTHUR SULLIVAN

1. On-ward, Christian sol - diers! Marching as to war, With the cross of
2. Like a might-y ar - my Moves the Church of God; Brothers, we are
3. Crowns and thrones may perish, Kingdoms rise and wane; But the Church of
4. On-ward, then, ye peo - ple! Join our happy throng; Blend with ours your

Je - sus Go - ing on be - fore; Christ, the roy - al Mas - ter,
tread - ing Where the saints have trod; We are not di - vid - ed,
Je - sus Con-stant will re - main; Gates of hell can nev - er
voic - es In the tri-umph song; Glo - ry, laud, and hon - or,

Leads a-gainst the foe; For-ward in - to bat - tle, See, His banners go!
All one bod - y we; One in hope and doc - trine, One in char - i - ty.
'Gainst that Church prevail; We have Christ's own promise, Which can never fail.
Un - to Christ the King; This thro' countless a - ges Men and an - gels sing.

CHORUS

On-ward, Chris-tian sol - diers! March-ing as to war,

With the cross of Je - sus Go - ing on be - fore.

Dare to Be a Daniel

P. P. B.

P. P. Bliss

1. Stand-ing by a pur-pose true, Heed-ing God's command, Hon-or them, the
2. Man-y might-y men are lost, Dar-ing not to stand, Who for God had
3. Man-y gi-ants, great and tall, Stalk-ing thro' the land, Headlong to the
4. Hold the gos-pel ban-ner high! On to vic-t'ry grand! Sa-tan and His

Chorus

faith-ful few! All hail to Dan-iel's Band!
been a host, By join-ing Dan-iel's Band! Dare to be a Dan-iel,
earth would fall, If met by Dan-iel's Band!
host de-fy, And shout for Dan-iel's Band!

Dare to stand a-lone! Dare to have a pur-pose firm! Dare to make it known!

Children of the Heavenly King

Rev John Cennick.

Arr. from Ignace Pleyel.

1. Chil-dren of the heav'n-ly King, As ye jour-ney, sweet-ly sing;
2. We are trav-'ling home to God, In the way the fa-thers trod:
3. Fear not, breth-ren, joy-ful stand On the bor-ders of your land;
4. Lord, o-be-dient-ly we go, Glad-ly leav-ing all be-low;

Children of the Heavenly King

Sing your Sav-ior's wor - thy praise, Glo-rious in His works and ways.
They are hap-py now, and we Soon their hap-pi - ness shall see.
Je - sus Christ, your Fa-ther's Son, Bids you un - dis-mayed go on.
On - ly Thou our Lead - er be, And we still will fol - low Thee. A-MEN.

Jesus Bids Us Shine

E. O. EXCELL

1. Je - sus bids us shine, With a clear, pure light, Like a lit - tle
2. Je - sus bids us shine, First of all for Him; Well He sees and
3. Je - sus bids us shine, Then, for all a - round Man - y kinds of
4. Je - sus bids us shine, As we work for Him, Bring-ing those that

can - dle Burn - ing in the night; In this world of dark - ness
knows it If our light is dim; He looks down from heav - en,
dark-ness In this world a - bound— Sin, and want, and sor - row:
wan - der From the paths of sin; He will ev - er help us,

We must shine, You in your small cor - ner, And I in mine.
Sees us shine, You in your small cor - ner, And I in mine.
We must shine, You in your small cor - ner, And I in mine.
If we shine, You in your small cor - ner, And I in mine.

Jesus Loves the Little Children

Rev. C. H. Woolston, D. D.

Geo. F. Root

1. Je-sus calls the chil-dren dear, "Come to Me and nev-er fear, For I
2. Je-sus is the Shep-herd true, And He'll al-ways stand by you, For He
3. I am com-ing, Lord, to Thee, And Thy sol-dier I will be, For He

love the lit-tle chil-dren of the world; I will take you by the hand,
loves the lit-tle chil-dren of the world; He's a Sav-ior great and strong,
loves the lit-tle chil-dren of the world; And His cross I'll al-ways bear,

Lead you to the bet-ter land, For I love the lit-tle
And He'll shield you from the wrong, For He loves the lit-tle
And for Him I'll do and dare, For He loves the lit-tle

CHORUS

chil-dren of the world."
chil-dren of the world.   Je-sus loves the lit-tle chil - dren,
chil-dren of the world.   lit-tle chil-dren,

All the chil-dren of the world;   Red and yel-low, black and white, They are
All the chil - dren   of the world;

Jesus Loves the Little Children

pre-cious in His sight, Je-sus loves the lit-tle chil-dren of the world.

What a Friend

JOSEPH SCRIVEN

CHARLES C. CONVERSE

1. What a Friend we have in Je-sus, All our sins and griefs to bear!
2. Have we tri-als and temp-ta-tions? Is there troub-le an-y-where?
3. Are we weak and heav-y-la-den, Cumbered with a load of care?—

What a priv-i-lege to car-ry Ev-'ry-thing to God in prayer!
We should nev-er be dis-cour-aged, Take it to the Lord in prayer.
Pre-cious Sav-ior, still our ref-uge,—Take it to the Lord in prayer.

O what peace we oft-en for-feit, O what need-less pain we bear,
Can we find a friend so faith-ful Who will all our sor-rows share?
Do thy friends despise, for-sake thee? Take it to the Lord in prayer;

All be-cause we do not car-ry Ev-'ry-thing to God in prayer!
Je-sus knows our ev-'ry weak-ness, Take it to the Lord in prayer.
In His arms He'll take and shield thee, Thou wilt find a sol-ace there.

Count Your Blessings

Rev. Johnson Oatman, Jr.

E. O. Excell

1. When up-on life's bil-lows you are tem-pest-tossed, When you are dis-
2. Are you ev-er bur-dened with a load of care? Does the cross seem
3. When you look at oth-ers with their lands and gold, Think that Christ has
4. So, a-mid the con-flict, whether great or small, Do not be dis-

cour-aged, think-ing all is lost, Count your man-y bless-ings, name them
heav-y you are called to bear? Count your man-y bless-ings, ev-'ry
prom-ised you His wealth un-told; Count your man-y bless-ings, mon-ey
cour-aged, God is o-ver all; Count your man-y bless-ings, an-gels

one by one, And it will sur-prise you what the Lord hath done.
doubt will fly, And you will be sing-ing as the days go by.
can-not buy Your re-ward in heav-en, nor your home on high.
will at-tend, Help and com-fort give you to your jour-ney's end.

Chorus.

Count your bless-ings, Name them one by one; Count your
Count your man-y bless-ings, Name them one by one; Count your man-y

bless-ings, See what God hath done; Count your bless-ings,
bless-ings, See what God hath done; Count your man-y bless-ings,

Count Your Blessings

Name them one by one; Count your man-y blessings, See what God hath done.

Jesus Loves Me

Anna B. Warner, alt.   Wm. B. Bradbury

1. Je - sus loves me! this I know, For the Bi - ble tells me so; Lit - tle
2. Je - sus loves me! loves me still, Tho' I'm ver - y weak and ill; That I
3. Je - sus loves me! He who died, Heaven's gate to o - pen wide; He will
4. Je - sus loves me! He will stay Close be - side me all the way; Thou hast

ones to Him be-long; They are weak, but He is strong.
might from sin be free, Bled and died up - on the tree. Yes, Je - sus loves me!
wash a - way my sin, Let His lit - tle child come in.
bled and died for me, I will hence-forth live for Thee.

Chorus

Yes, Je - sus loves me! Yes, Je - sus loves me! The Bi - ble tells me so.

I Love to Tell the Story

CATHERINE HANKEY

WILLIAM G. FISCHER

1. I love to tell the story Of un-seen things a-bove, Of
2. I love to tell the story, More won-der-ful it seems Than
3. I love to tell the story, 'Tis pleas-ant to re-peat What
4. I love to tell the story, For those who know it best Seem

Je-sus and His glo-ry, Of Je-sus and His love. I love to
all the gold-en fan-cies Of all our gold-en dreams. I love to
seems, each time I tell it, More won-der-ful-ly sweet. I love to
hun-ger-ing and thirst-ing To hear it like the rest. And when, in

tell the sto-ry, Be-cause I know 'tis true; It sat-is-fies my
tell the sto-ry, It did so much for me; And that is just the
tell the sto-ry, For some have nev-er heard The mes-sage of sal-
scenes of glo-ry, I sing the new, new song, 'Twill be the old, old

CHORUS

longings As noth-ing else can do.
rea-son I tell it now to thee. I love to tell the sto-ry, 'Twill
va-tion From God's own ho-ly Word.
sto-ry That I have loved so long.

be my theme in glo-ry To tell the old, old sto-ry Of Jesus and His love.

260

America the Beautiful

The Star-Spangled Banner

FRANCIS SCOTT KEY

1. Oh,   say, can you see, by the dawn's ear-ly light, What so proud-ly we
2. On the shore, dim-ly seen thro' the mists of the deep, Where the foe's haughty
3. And where is that band, who so vaunt-ing-ly swore That the hav - oc of
4. Oh,   thus be it   ev - er when free-men shall stand Be - tween their loved

hailed at the twilight's last gleaming? Whose broad stripes and bright stars, thro' the
host   in dread si-lence re-pos - es, What   is   that which the breeze, o'er the
war   and the bat-tle's con-fu - sion, A   home and a coun - try should
homes and the war's des - o - la - tion; Blest with vic - t'ry and peace, may the

per - il - ous fight, O'er the ramparts we watched, were so gal-lant-ly stream-ing?
tow - er-ing steep, As   it fit - ful - ly blows, half conceals, half dis-clos - es?
leave us no more? Their   blood has washed out their foul footsteps' pol-lu-tion;
Heav'n-rescued land Praise the Pow'r that hath made and preserved us a na - tion!

And the rock-ets' red glare, the bombs bursting in air,   Gave proof thro' the
Now it catch-es the gleam of the morning's first beam, In full glo - ry re-
No   ref-uge could save the   hire-ling and slave From the ter - ror of
Then   con-quer we must, when our cause it is just;   And this be our

The Star-Spangled Banner

night that our flag was still there. Oh, say, does that star-span-gled
flect - ed, now shines on the stream: 'Tis the star-span-gled ban - ner; oh,
flight or the gloom of the grave. And the star-span-gled ban - ner in
mot - to: "In God is our trust!" And the star-span-gled ban - ner in

ban - ner yet wave O'er the land of the free, and the home of the brave?
long may it wave O'er the land of the free, and the home of the brave.
tri - umph doth wave O'er the land of the free, and the home of the brave.
tri - umph shall wave O'er the land of the free, and the home of the brave.

America

S. F. SMITH

HENRY CAREY

1. My coun-try, 'tis of thee, Sweet land of lib - er - ty, Of thee I sing: Land where my
2. My na-tive coun-try, thee, Land of the no-ble free, Thy name I love: I love thy
3. Let mu-sic swell the breeze, And ring from all the trees Sweet freedom's song: Let mor-tal
4. Our fa-thers' God, to Thee, Au - thor of lib - er - ty, To Thee we sing: Long may our

fa - thers died, Land of the pil-grim's pride, From ev-'ry moun-tain side Let free-dom ring!
rocks and rills, Thy woods and templed hills; My heart with rapture thrills Like that a - bove.
tongues awake; Let all that breathe partake; Let rocks their silence break, The sound pro-long.
land be bright With freedom's ho - ly light; Pro-tect us by Thy might, Great God, our King!

The First Noel

Traditional   Traditional

1. The first No-el the angel did say Was to certain poor shepherds in fields as they lay;
2. And by the light of that same Star, Three wise men came from country far;
3. This Star drew nigh to the northwest, O'er Beth-le-hem it took its rest,
4. Then enter-ed in those wise men three, Full rev-'rent-ly up-on their knee,

In fields where they lay keeping their sheep, On a cold winter's night that was so deep.
To seek for a King was their in-tent, And to follow the Star wherever it went.
And there it did both stop and stay, Right o-ver the place where Jesus lay.
And of-fered there in His pres-ence, Their gold, and myrrh, and frank-incense.

REFRAIN.

No-el, No-el, No-el, No-el, Born is the King of Is-ra-el.

Silent Night

Joseph Mohr   P. M.   Franz Gruber

1. Si-lent night! ho-ly night! All is calm, all is bright 'Round yon
2. Si-lent night! ho-ly night! Shep-herds quake at the sight! Glo-ries
3. Si-lent night! ho-ly night! Son of God, love's pure light Ra-diant

Silent Night

vir - gin moth - er and Child! Ho - ly In-fant, so ten-der and mild,
stream from heaven a - far, Heav'n-ly hosts sing Al - le - lu - ia;
beams from Thy ho - ly face, With the dawn of re - deem - ing grace,

Sleep in heav - en - ly peace, Sleep in heav - en - ly peace.
Christ, the Sav - ior, is born, Christ, the Sav - ior, is born.
Je - sus, Lord, at Thy birth, Je - sus, Lord, at Thy birth. A - men.

Away in a Manger

Martin Luther

Martin Luther

1. A - way in a man - ger, No crib for a bed, The lit - tle Lord
2. The cat - tle are low - ing, The Ba - by a - wakes, But lit - tle Lord
3. Be near me, Lord Je - sus, I ask Thee to stay Close by me for-

Je - sus Laid down His sweet head; The stars in the sky Looked
Je - sus, No cry - ing He makes; I love Thee, Lord Je - sus! Look
ev - er, And love me, I pray; Bless all the dear chil-dren In

down where He lay,—The lit - tle Lord Je - sus, A - sleep on the hay.
down from the sky, And stay by my cra - dle, Till morn - ing is nigh.
Thy ten - der care, Pre - pare us for heav - en, To live with Thee there.

It Came upon the Midnight Clear

Edmund H. Sears   Richard S. Willis

1. It came up-on the mid-night clear, That glo-rious song of old,
2. Still thro' the clo-ven skies they come, With peace-ful wings un-furled,
3. And ye, be-neath life's crushing load, Whose forms are bend-ing low,
4. For lo, the days are has-t'ning on, By proph-et bards fore-told,

From an-gels bend-ing near the earth To touch their harps of gold:
And still their heav'n-ly mu-sic floats O'er all the wea-ry world:
Who toil a-long the climb-ing way With pain-ful steps and slow,
When with the ev-er-cir-cling years Comes round the age of gold;

"Peace on the earth, good-will to men, From heav'n's all-gracious King:" The
A-bove its sad and low-ly plains They bend on hov'ring wing: And
Look now! for glad and gold-en hours Come swift-ly on the wing; O
When peace shall o-ver all the earth Its an-cient splen-dors fling, And

world in sol-emn still-ness lay To hear the an-gels sing.
ev-er o'er its Ba-bel sounds The bless-ed an-gels sing.
rest be-side the wea-ry road, And hear the an-gels sing.
the whole world give back the song Which now the an-gels sing. A-MEN.

PRAYERS
FOR
BOYS
AND
GIRLS

When I Wake Up

Thank You, God, for the morn-
    ing,
For the birds and flowers and
    trees.
Thank You for the shining sun
That shines its warmth on me.
Thank You for mommy and
    daddy,
And bless them, God, I pray,
And please, God, be with us
To share a happy day.

      Amen

Thoughts for Today

I will do my best to make this day a happy one in every way. I hope
I please You, God, in everything I do and say. Do help me, God, to
live each one according to Your plan, and bless my mommy and daddy
for teaching me Your ways.

      Amen

Dear God,
Please bless our house
And everything we have.
Give us what is good for us,
And take away the bad.

    Amen

A Place to Worship

Thank You, God, for Your
    church;
It's there we worship You and
    sing.
Thank You, God, for loving us.
I thank You for everything!

    Amen

Dear God,
Bless every child of Yours this
    day;
Help us to be grateful.
Teach us Your Truth, O Lord,
Inspire us to be faithful.
                Amen

Dear God!

Help me not to be afraid
Of things I don't understand.
Please, God, be near me always
And lead me by the hand.
                Amen

Things Jesus Taught

Dear God,
Sometimes, when I have a self-
    ish thought,
I have trouble remembering
    what Jesus taught:
"It is more blessed to give than
    receive."
Sometimes, when I get angry,
    and have a bitter thought,
I have trouble remembering
    what Jesus taught:
"Blessed are the meek."
Lord, help me to be humble,
    help me to be pure in heart.
                Amen

City of Glory

Dear God, I think of You so far away, Beyond the clouds in Heaven, a beautiful city to behold, complete with golden mansions. Jesus sits at Your right hand, in a white and shining robe; directing the universe and watching all His children. Teach me Your ways, dear Lord, and prepare me for Your glorious Kingdom.
                Amen

Beginning a New Day

Dear God,
Thank You for this new day.
When You light the sky with
Your bright sun,
I know a brand new day's be-
gun.
I do thank You, God, for each
and every one.

Amen

A Morning Prayer

Thank You, God,
For a restful night.
And thank You for the morn-
ing light.
Please help me to have a happy
day,
And all the friends with whom
I play.

Amen

Love of God and Family

Dear God, Thank You for my family, I love my dad and mother. You
gave me a little sister, and also a baby brother. It's so good to have
You with us, God, loving us as You do. Help us all to share that love;
sister, brother, dad and mom. Remember God, we love You, too!

Amen

Wonders to Behold

Dear God,
Thank You for all you've
made,
The earth, the grass, the trees,
The rolling hills, the deep blue
lakes,
The winding rivers and the
streams.
You created the soothing rain
And every gentle breeze.
Thank You so much, dear God,
For all these wonderful things.

Amen

Thank You for Everything

Thank You, God, for light,
Thank You for my friends.
Thank You, God, for eyes
to see
All the pretty flowers
and trees.
Thank You for my toys
I share,
Thank You, God, for play.
I thank You, God, for every-
thing
Each and every day.

Amen

A Prayer for Animals

Dear God, Please bless animals everywhere—especially those who have no home, and no one to feed or care for them; the birds and the bunnies, kittens and puppies; and don't forget big dogs, too; horses and cows, and all the farm animals. I pray You will bless them all the same.

Amen

A Blessing

Dear God,
You make it possible for plants
  to grow.
You provide our daily food,
The water we drink, and every
  good thing,
You know.
Help us, God, to look to You
For all our needs each day,
With Your Spirit of Love
  in us,
Spreading joy in every way.

Amen

An Evening Prayer

Dear God, I tried this day to
  do my best
And now, I thank You for my
  rest.
Please be with all children
  everywhere,
To share Your tender loving
  Care.
And bless my mommy and
  daddy, too,
For they have taught me love
  for You.

Amen

Great Bible Truths

BLESSED ARE THE RIGHTEOUS

Blessed is the man that walketh not
 in the counsel of the ungodly,
 nor standeth in the way of sinners,
 nor sitteth in the seat of the scornful.
But his delight is in the law of the Lord;
 and in his law doth he meditate
 day and night.
And he shall be like a tree
 planted by the rivers of water,
 that bringeth forth his fruit in his season;
 his leaf also shall not wither;
 and whatsoever he doeth shall prosper.

The ungodly are not so:
 but are like the chaff
 which the wind driveth away.
Therefore the ungodly shall not
 stand in the judgment,
 nor sinners in the congregation
 of the righteous.
For the Lord knoweth the way
 of the righteous:
 but the way of the ungodly shall perish.

Psalm 1

THE SHEPHERD'S PSALM

The Lord is my Shepherd; I shall not want.

He maketh me to lie down in green pastures:
    he leadeth me beside the still waters.

He restoreth my soul:
    he leadeth me in the paths of righteousness
    for his name's sake.

Yea, though I walk through the valley
    of the shadow of death,
        I will fear no evil: for thou art with me;
        thy rod and thy staff they comfort me.

Thou preparest a table before me in the presence
    of mine enemies: thou anointest my head
    with oil; my cup runneth over.

Surely goodness and mercy shall follow me all the
    days of my life: and I will dwell in the
    house of the Lord for ever.

Psalm 23

THE TEN COMMANDMENTS

I

Thou shalt have no other gods
before me.

II

Thou shalt not make unto thee any
graven image.

III

Thou shalt not take the name of the
Lord thy God in vain.

IV

Remember the sabbath day, to
keep it holy.

V

Honor thy father and thy mother.

VI

Thou shalt not kill.

VII

Thou shalt not commit adultery.

VIII

Thou shalt not steal.

IX

Thou shalt not bear false witness.

X

Thou shalt not covet.

Exodus 20:3-17

THE BEATITUDES

Blessed are the poor in spirit: for theirs is the
      kingdom of heaven.

Blessed are they that mourn: for they shall
      be comforted.

Blessed are the meek: for they shall inherit
      the earth.

Blessed are they which do hunger and thirst after
      righteousness: for they shall be filled.

Blessed are the merciful: for they shall
      obtain mercy.

Blessed are the pure in heart: for they shall
      see God.

Blessed are the peacemakers: for they shall be
      called the children of God.

Blessed are they which are persecuted for
      righteousness' sake: for theirs is the
      kingdom of heaven.

Blessed are ye, when men shall revile you, and
      persecute you, and shall say all manner of
      evil against you falsely, for my sake.

Rejoice, and be exceeding glad: for great is your
      reward in heaven: for so persecuted they
      the prophets which were before you.

Matthew 5:3-12

THE LORD'S PRAYER

Our Father which art in heaven,
    Hallowed be thy name.

Thy kingdom come.

Thy will be done
    in earth, as it is in heaven.

Give us this day our daily bread.

And forgive us our debts,
    as we forgive our debtors.

And lead us not into temptation,
    but deliver us from evil:
        For thine is the kingdom, and the
    power, and the glory, for ever.

Amen.

Matthew 6:9-13

THE GREATEST
OF THESE IS LOVE

Though I speak with the tongues of men and of angels, and have not love, I am become as sounding brass, or a tinkling cymbal.

And though I have the gift of prophecy, and understand all mysteries, and all knowledge; and though I have all faith, so that I could remove mountains, and have not love, I am nothing.

And though I bestow all my goods to feed the poor, and though I give my body to be burned, and have not love, it profiteth me nothing.

Love suffereth long, and is kind; love envieth not; love vaunteth not itself, is not puffed up,

Doth not behave itself unseemly, seeketh not her own, is not easily provoked, thinketh no evil;

Rejoiceth not in iniquity, but rejoiceth in the truth;

Beareth all things, believeth all things, hopeth all
things, endureth all things.

Love never faileth: but whether there be prophecies,
they shall fail; whether there be tongues,
they shall cease; whether there be
knowledge, it shall vanish away.

For we know in part, and we prophesy in part.

But when that which is perfect is come, then that
which is in part shall be done away.

When I was a child, I spake as a child,
I understood as a child, I thought as a
child: but when I became a man,
I put away childish things.

For now we see through a glass, darkly; but then
face to face: now I know in part; but then
shall I know even as also I am known.

And now abideth faith, hope, love, these three;
but the greatest of these is love.

I Corinthians 13:1-13

THE LOVE OF GOD

For God so loved the world, that he gave his only begotten Son, that whosoever believeth in him should not perish, but have everlasting life.

John 3:16

THE TWO GREATEST COMMANDMENTS

Master, which is the great commandment in the law?

Jesus said unto him,

Thou shalt love the Lord thy God with all thy heart, and with all thy soul, and with all thy mind.

This is the first and great commandment.

And the second is like unto it,

Thou shalt love thy neighbor as thyself.

Matthew 22:36-39

JESUS SAID:

Go ye therefore, and teach all nations, baptizing them in the name of the Father, and of the Son, and of the Holy Ghost:

Teaching them to observe all things whatsoever I have commanded you: and, lo, I am with you alway, even unto the end of the world.

Amen.

Matthew 28:19-20

GOD'S PROMISE OF STRENGTH

But they that wait upon the Lord
shall renew their strength; they shall
mount up with wings as eagles; they shall
run, and not be weary; and they shall walk,
and not faint.

Isaiah 40:31

GOD'S GLORY AND MAN'S HONOR

When I consider thy heavens, the work
of thy fingers,
the moon and the stars, which thou
hast ordained;
what is man, that thou art mindful
of him?
and the son of man, that thou visitest him?

For thou hast made him a little lower
than the angels,
and hast crowned him with glory and honor.

Psalm 8:3-5

THE FIRST COMING

And she brought forth her firstborn son,
and wrapped him in swaddling clothes,
and laid him in a manger; because there was
no room for them in the inn.

Luke 2:7

And Jesus said unto him, Foxes have holes
and birds of the air have nests;
but the Son of man hath not where to
lay his head.

Luke 9:58

Him, being delivered by the determinate
counsel and foreknowledge of God, ye have
taken, and by wicked hands have
crucified and slain:

Acts 2:23

THE SECOND COMING

And they shall see the Son of man
coming in the clouds of heaven
with power and great glory.   *Matthew 24:30*

his eyes were as a flame of fire,
and on his head were many crowns;...
and he hath on his vesture and on his thigh
a name written, King of Kings, and
Lord of Lords.   *Revelation 19:12, 16*

the kingdoms of this world are become the
kingdoms of our Lord, and of his Christ;
and he shall reign for ever and ever.

Revelation 11:15

JESUS THE WAY TO THE FATHER

Let not your heart be troubled: ye believe in God,
     believe also in me.
In my Father's house are many mansions:
     if it were not so, I would have told you.
I go to prepare a place for you.

And if I go and prepare a place for you,
     I will come again, and receive you unto myself;
     that where I am, there ye may be also.

John 14:1-3

THE GREAT INVITATION

Come unto me, all ye that labor and are
     heavy laden, and I will give you rest.
Take my yoke upon you, and learn of me;
     for I am meek and lowly in heart:
     and ye shall find rest unto your souls.
For my yoke is easy, and
     my burden is light.

Matthew 11:28-30

A PSALM OF PRAISE

Make a joyful noise unto the Lord,
    all ye lands.
Serve the Lord with gladness:
    come before his presence with singing.
Know ye that the Lord he is God:
    it is he that hath made us,
    and not we ourselves;
    we are his people, and the sheep
    of his pasture.
Enter into his gates with thanksgiving,
    and into his courts with praise:
    be thankful unto him,
    and bless his name.
For the Lord is good; his mercy is everlasting;
    and his truth endureth to all generations.

Psalm 100